A lemon shark feeding.

ALSO by CAPTAIN HAL SCHARP:

Florida's Game Fish and How To Land Them

Shark Safari

Shark Safari

Captain Hal Scharp

SOUTH BRUNSWICK AND NEW YORK: A. S. BARNES AND COMPANY
LONDON: THOMAS YOSELOFF LTD.

A. S. Barnes and Co., Inc.
Cranbury, New Jersey 08512

Thomas Yoseloff Ltd.
108 New Bond Street
London W1Y OQX, England

Library of Congress Cataloging in Publication Data

Scharp, Hal.
    Shark safari.

    Bibliography: p.
    1. Sharks.   2. Shark fishing   I. Title
QL638.9.S28   597'.31   73-22602
ISBN 0-498-01459-2

PRINTED IN THE UNITED STATES OF AMERICA

Now that he is of use to man, may his
numbers not grow appreciably less!
Captain William E. Young
Shark! Shark!, 1933

Contents

Preface

AS LONG AS I CAN REMEMBER, I HAVE BEEN INTERESTED IN THE SEA AND intrigued by its many strange creatures. The shark, in particular, has always created a special excitement in me, one that became so absorbing that I finally *had* to experiment and study its capricious behavior and biological construction. A good portion of this book represents the culmination of my experiences and studies—the result of an obsessive quest that still continues.

Gliding silently among the oceans of the world are approximately 250 scientifically classified species of sharks. As a group their distribution is worldwide, but the great majority inhabit the tropical and subtropical zones. Many of this number (except for very slight variances in anatomy) are so incredibly similar in appearance that only a qualified ichthyologist can distinguish between them. Sometimes even the experts disagree and often reach an impasse while determining a shark's identity. Most of the species are rarely encountered and a great number of them might never be found in a lifetime of searching. For these reasons, I have discriminated in my selection and chosen to discuss those common species that the reader is more likely to meet. In some instances, I have compromised a little and included a few rare species whose unusual characteristics or behavior may intrigue and entertain the reader. Essentially, all aspects of sharks will be reviewed—as menaces to society, biological curiosities, aids in medical research, challenges to an angler, or a means of making a living.

The shark's universal reputation for eating people is an evil one, stemming from ancient accounts of shark attacks. Many are legendary and grossly exaggerated. Yet, for thousands of years, the sight of a dorsal fin cutting the water's surface has chilled men's spines and caused their flesh to creep. Although present-day records are more accurate, the shark is still a symbol of terror. But, statistically, man's chances or survival are better in the sea than when he is dodging the rush-hour traffic in any large city of the world!

As I began a close examination of this impetuous, hostile sea wolf, a marvelously constructed creature was revealed: biologically, the perfect digestive and reproductive machine; aesthetically, an animal of exquisite grace and terrible beauty. Its adaptation to severe changes in environment during 300 million years of evolution is astonishing. No other vertebral creature reached such dizzy heights of evolutionary success. As I tried to penetrate the mysteries of this creature's origin and biological structure, I was awed by its ability to survive and amazed at its remarkable physiological functions.

This book also depicts our reaction to the shark's incongruous and peculiar temperament and what is being done about it. It describes how we utilize the shark for the advancement of medical science and how we distribute its marketable properties. Although the business world is aware of the economic potential offered by the shark, a wide hiatus still exists between the scientific community and progressive industry. One day this gap will be bridged by new concepts of commercial application.

I have endeavored to present an honest portrait of this greatly maligned and enigmatic creature—one of the oldest predators in the sea, one whose legends tend to obscure the truth about him and his hunters, whose odysseys have taken them to the unexplored regions of the earth.

Because the shark is an extremely provocative and mysterious animal, it has become an international celebrity and a subject of strong controversy. Unfortunately, some writers, who have never experienced a personal encounter with a shark, rashly used their narrative powers to describe the creature's character and physiological structure. Filling their chronicles with generalizations and misleading facts, twisting and contorting legend and science, they certainly have not illuminated the shark's true, elusive character.

I realize that a subject such as this is so vast in its scope that many shortcomings may be present throughout the material. In spite of this possible deficit, I hope that the reader will enjoy his "safari" into the awesome world of the shark and will share my fascination for one of the most mysterious and unpredictable creatures in the animal kingdom.

Acknowledgments

PROBABLY ONE OF A WRITER'S GREATEST FEARS, AFTER COMPLETING
systematic research and committing his findings and evaluations to
paper, is that he may have neglected to mention those who gave their
time and material so generously. Without their cooperation, this book
could not have been written. Therefore, I have made a particular
point to acknowledge their efforts and hope that I have made no
omissions.

No one has given greater help and inspiration in the preparation of
this manuscript than my wife, Mary. Although I had begun this enormous project before I met her, she jumped right in with enthusiasm
and joined me in numerous research adventures. Later, as the manuscript began to take form, I realized I couldn't let her talent in editing
and proofing get away; so, I decided to "keep it in the family." To her
I owe my first acknowledgment—with love.

During the course of research, it is necessary to draw upon many
sources for information that must be evaluated, checked, and double-
checked for authenticity and accuracy. This means soliciting the
cooperation of many people, agencies, and scientific organizations. For
their wonderful cooperation and practical assistance, I owe a deep debt
of gratitude to the following: Dr. Perry Gilbert, Chairman of the Shark
Research Panel of the American Institute of Biological Sciences and
Executive Director of the Mote Marine Laboratory, Sarasota, Florida;
Mr. Morris M. Vorenberg, President of the Palm Beach Sharkers, Inc.,
West Palm Beach, Florida, and shark attack investigator for the Shark
Research Panel, American Institute of Biological Sciences; Dr. John
G. Casey, Narragansett Sport Fisheries Marine Laboratory, Rhode
Island; Dr. John H. Heller, President and Executive Director of the
New England Institute for Medical Research, Ridgefield, Connecticut;
Dr. Eugenie Clark, University of Maryland; and Mr. Raymond D.
Hetterick, President, Lakeside Laboratories, Milwaukee, Wisconsin.

A big vote of thanks goes to Captain Frank Mundus of Montauk,
New York, who furnished action photographs and material relative to
his profession of sportfishing for sharks; to Mr. Cecil Jacobs of the

Durban Shark Angling Club, South Africa, for contributing photographs and the special methods they use in catching sharks from piers; to Mr. John Papavero, President of the Gulf Coast Sharkers, St. Petersburg, Florida, for furnishing photographs and procedures pertaining to sharkfishing along Florida's west coast; to Mr. Ernest Palmer, of South Australia and representative of the International Game Fish Association, for his personal experiences, photographs, and methods used in catching record great white sharks in Australian waters; to Mr. Hamish Rogerson, Secretary, Shark Angling Club of Great Britain, for his generous assistance in supplying complete information pertaining to his club's activities and accommodations; and to the staff of the International Game Fish Association who have cooperated by keeping me up-to-date on record catches held by shark anglers.

I am particularly indebted to the competent staffs of the following government agencies and research institutions: Fish and Wildlife Service, U. S. Department of Interior; International Oceanographic Foundation, Miami, Florida; Woods Hole Oceanographic Institution, Woods Hole, Massachusetts; Smithsonian Institution, Washington, D. C.; Mote Marine Laboratory, Sarasota, Florida; Oceanographic Research Institute, Durban, South Africa; and the U. S. Naval Undersea Research and Development Center, San Diego, California.

My sincere thanks to: Captain Les Rayen, President of the Tiburon Industries, Fort Pierce, Florida, for the opportunity to join him on his commercial shark-fishing excursions and to report my observations of his operation; to Gerrit Klay, President of Shark-Quarium, Grassy Key, Florida, for information and photographs dealing with his method of transporting live sharks; and to Captain William B. Gray, Director of Collections and Exhibitions at Seaquarium in Miami, Florida, for his excellent photographs.

My gratitude is boundless for the invaluable assistance of: Mr. Des Brennan, Organizing Controller, The Inland Fisheries Trust Incorporated, Ireland, for the information and excellent photographs that portray the shark-fishing activity in the British Isles; Mr. Al Pflueger, Jr., Taxidermist, Hallendale, Florida, for photographs and data relative to the mounting of sharks; and to Mr. Gerard R. Case, Jersey City, New Jersey, who is well qualified in his specialized field of paleontology. He has been generous in providing photographs and information relating to his studies of primitive sharks.

Since my penmanship is atrocious, I salute Mrs. Phyllis Lademann. Her uncanny ability to decipher my scribbling and to convert it into a beautifully typed manuscript is greatly appreciated.

Finally, I must acknowledge my indebtedness to the many anglers throughout the world who have caught official world-record sharks. The following have been extremely cooperative in contributing personal accounts of their extraordinary angling achievements and photographs from their private collections—all of which went into the exciting chapter These are the Champs: Mr. Alfred Dean of South Australia; Mr. and Mrs. Bob Dyer of South Australia; Mr. Walter Maxwell of Charlotte, North Carolina; Mr. Des Bougourd of Guernsey, Channel Islands; Captain Ray Acord of Agana, Guam; Mr. Barry Caldwell of New South Wales, Australia; Miss Helen Gillis of New South Wales, Australia; Mr. Del Marsh of Long Beach, California; and Mr. Doug Ross of Whangarei, New Zealand.

And I am grateful to my many customers. Because of their enthusiasm and participation in shark-fishing, I have been able to share their experiences and to record in this book some of the many thrilling, memorable episodes that took place aboard my boat.

Shark Safari

1
Spectres Out of the Past

SCIENTISTS ESTIMATE THAT OUR PLANET EARTH IS ROUGHLY FOUR AND one half billion years old. Since its birth it has undergone countless major physical changes that have greatly altered its external structure and climate. It is still changing today, although long periods of time must elapse before man can recognize any significant alteration.

Experts can read the graphic story of the earth's history in the stratified layers of rock that make up the earth's mantle. From the study of rocks they have discovered that the earliest life forms appeared over a billion years ago. It was the very lowest form of life and as such it no longer exists, but its inception started a steady procession of living creatures that began their perilous ascent up the evolutionary ladder. Some of these extraordinary creatures were able to develop gradually and were enhanced by environmental changes, while others became extinct because they were unable to adapt to the slow but persistent modifications taking place in their surroundings.

Eons later, approximately 480 million years ago during the Devonian period, the first sharklike fish appeared. Since most fossil records are incomplete, there are considerable mysteries surrounding the shark's origin. Recent fossil discoveries have provided paleontologists with reasonably accurate estimates about the creature's period of existence during the prehistoric era, but there are still many "missing links" to be uncovered.

Unlike primitive fishes whose vertebral structure lends itself conveniently to fossilization, the shark's skeleton is composed of calcified cartilage—prone to attack by bacteria. This bacterial process destroys most of the structures we would like to study.

In the Cleveland, Ohio, Devonian mud shales underlying that city, important studies have been conducted that have pinpointed the existence and time of some of the earliest primitive sharks. The age of these early sharklike fish dates back more than 400 million years. From the body outlines of the sharks, *Cladoselache* and its allied species (*Ctenacanth* and *Pleuracanth*), paleontologists were able to reconstruct sharks from one and one half to four feet in length. These discoveries at Cleveland are considered the most valuable records of the earliest sharklike fish forms on earth.

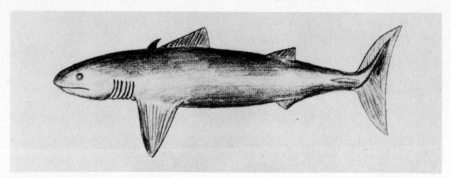

One of the earliest primitive sharks, Cladoselache, *thrived during the Devonian period more than 350 million years ago. The drawing illustrates the restoration of the sharklike fossil found in the mud shales of Cleveland, Ohio.*

The transition from earlier jawless armored fishes to the sharklike fishes was slow but deliberate, as nature gradually converted the bony exoskeleton of the primitive jawless placoderm fishes to cartilage. To some extent, even the so-called bony fishes were partly cartilaginous— although they did eventually evolve to more solid bony structures—while the shark retained the primitive cartilaginous form. The shark eventually developed jaws with teeth from the forward part of its gill arch support bar, together with many other features that showed an evolution from placodermal beginnings.

During the last 300 million years, the earth has continued to undergo tremendous climatic changes. As its crust expanded and contracted huge fissures were created, while massive formations of sediment rose from the depths of the oceans and thrust their pinnacles skyward. Oceans flooded continents as rain and sea made intrusions upon the land. Strong currents swept over the land masses causing severe erosion and the formation of deep lakes and rivers. Great convulsions shook the earth and it trembled as huge mountain ranges were formed and snaked their way across continents while volcanic eruptions belched dense clouds of smoke and moisture. In some areas, huge land masses smoldered as steam hissed from their newly formed fissures made by gigantic fractures in the earth's crust.

In the primordial sea, the underwater landscape also underwent intense upheavals as the ocean bottom took on different shapes. Currents were rerouted continually by newly formed underseas mountain ranges and the development of ridges which, in turn, created deep trenches and vast plateaus. These great rearrangements in the earth's surface and ocean bottom took place frequently and caused countless numbers of living things to perish. Plant and animal life struggled helplessly for survival but many were unable to adjust to these severe conditions. It was indeed a very hazardous place for any living creature when it was caught in one of those many periods undergoing drastic environmental changes.

At the close of the Cenozoic era, when the ice ages began, (advancing and retreating throughout thousands of years during the Pleistocene epoch) severe climatic changes occured when tropic environments were engulfed by arctic chill. Great glacial ice sheets pushed down into the temperate zone, trapping and destroying all kinds of living plants and animals. Sea creatures too were annihilated as tropical waters cooled.

However, the sharks survived because of their incredible ability to thrive and develop. They took these major catastrophies in stride and adapted quickly to a new and cruel environment, while their neighbors became unfortunate victims of nature's brutal selectivity.

During the Mesozoic era (better known as the age of the reptiles), sharks existed in great abundance. It was a time when the giant dinosaurs ruled supreme for well over 100 million years. These prehistoric monsters trampled the earth's steaming swamps and tundra while their cousins, the giant sea-going reptiles (ichtyosaurs, plesiosaurs, and mosasaurs), pursued sharks, other fishes, and invertebrates in the oceans. Yet the sharks endured predators and a changing world as they persistently evolved.

According to some evolutionists, primitive and modern sharks have actually defied Darwin's theory of the survival of the fittest and the principle of natural selectivity. The success of a creature's perpetuation is not only in its ability to survive continuous and drastic environmental changes but also in its capacity to outsize, outnumber, and outwit other species that may threaten its survival. The shark falls short of these requirements and (according to Darwin's premise) should have failed in its evolutionary rise.

In comparison with other creatures, the shark's brain is and always has been a small and poorly developed organ and, therefore, the ability to outwit other predators is not one of its talents. The shark's size also had little to do with its ability to survive. Perhaps its successful survival depended upon the fact that it existed in great numbers. But one thing is certain, physiologically the shark was and is a more highly successful form of life than other primitive creatures, and that accounts for its continued existence through the ages.

The first sharklike fishes were probably direct descendants of the primitive placoderm fishes (discussed earlier), which flourished from the late Silurian to the late Devonian periods.

During the Devonian period (known as the age of the fishes) many fishes (both bony and cartilaginous) existed in the seas. The largest of these was *Dinichthys* ("terrible fish"). This monster was feared by all the sea creatures including the earliest sharklike fishes: *Cladose-lache, Ctenacanthus, Orodus,* and *Pleuracanthus. Dinichthys* grew to 20 feet in length and had an armored head and powerful beaklike jaws. During the latter part of the Devonian the first sharklike fishes appeared and their descendants existed into the late Triassic, when they were replaced by the hybodont shark. The hybodonts eventually became extinct as the shark continued to develop structural modifications that made it more adaptable to its ever-changing surroundings. This resulted in a whole new family of species, which we call modern sharks. The beginning of this particular development took place sometime during the latter part of the Jurassic period, which began about 165 million years ago and lasted for 30 million years. It was towards the end of the Cenozoic period (the Miocene epoch, 28 to 12 million years ago) that our present-day sharks became firmly established.

Sharks proliferated successfully and outnumbered most of the creatures in the sea. Included among the family that ranged the Miocene seas were other vertebrate creatures, such as the skates, rays, and the chimaeroids, who evolved with slightly different anatomical modifications. A few paleontologists still support the theory that the chimaeroids are not direct descendants of the shark but of a more primitive ancestor such as the placoderm.

Among the many species of sharks that flourished during the Miocene epoch, one genus—*Carcharodon*—mysteriously appeared. These were exceptionally large and one particular species, *Carcharodon megalodon,* was a huge monster that must have terrorized most of the inhabitants of the sea. This giant is the ancestor of our present-day great white shark, *Carcharodon carcharias.* We know that the dimensions of *C. megaladon* must have exceeded those of the giant dinosaurs or even our present-day whales that are usually considered the largest living creatures on earth.

The enormity of *C. megaladon* put it completely out of proportion to its sharky relatives. This sea-going goliath ruled its domain, since there were few other large predaceous creatures around at this time. Its appetite must have been enough to stagger anyone's imagination.

As far as we know from fossilized records, *C. megalodon's* only large contemporaries were the squalodonts. They were carnivorous whale-like mammals that did their share in terrorizing the inhabitants of the Miocene seas but since they were much smaller creatures, it is doubtful that squalodont posed a serious threat to *C. megaladon's* existence.

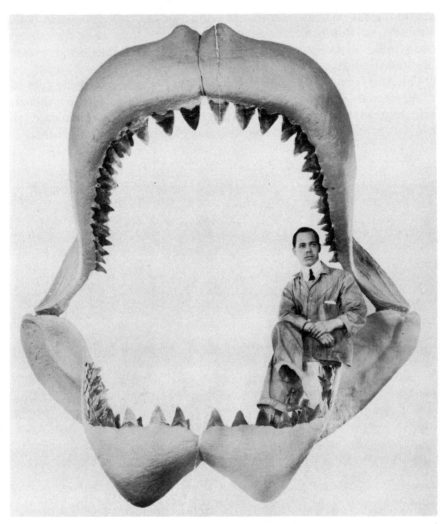

Using five- and six-inch fossil teeth, scientists reconstructed the jaws of Carcharodon megalodon, *a monstrous shark that roamed the Miocene seas 12 to 28 million years ago. From this particular jaw formation, it is speculated that the creature measured up to 75 feet in length. (Courtesy the American Museum of Natural History)*

It was probably the other way around. The squalodont whales were obviously no match for *C. megaladon's* six- to ten-foot jaws!

From *C. megaladon's* fossilized teeth, scientists have been able to determine when the creature existed and have speculated on its tremendous size. The range and distribution of the creature must have been extensive because its teeth have been found in fossil sites all over the world. These teeth, many of them measuring five to six inches in length, have been unearthed in the temperate and tropic zones of both hemispheres. Countless numbers of large teeth have been discovered along both coasts of the United States and have been uncovered several hundred miles from shore at the bottom of the ocean.

The American Museum of Natural History reconstructed the jaws of *C. megalodon* from fossilized teeth that measured five to six inches. The impressive jaws are so large that they can easily accommodate six full-grown, standing men! From this model, some paleontologists spec-

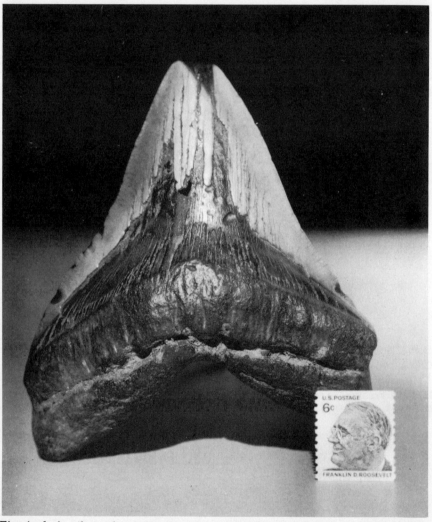

Five-inch fossil tooth of Carcharodon megalodon, *a direct ancestor of our present-day great white shark.* Carcharodon carcharias. *The tooth was found at Myrtle Beach, South Carolina.*

ulated that *C. megaladon* would have measured 60 to 80 feet in length. Others, less conservative, believe that the creature could have reached 100 feet or more!

There is no proof to substantiate the true size of this monster. But, he continues to grow as fresh excavations disclose larger teeth. Only recently, fossil teeth measuring seven and eight inches have been discovered in one of the phosphate pits of Polk County, Florida. Local fossil hunters even claim that a tooth "the size of a dinner plate" has been uncovered in this location. Although this particular discovery still lacks positive authentication, the seven- and eight-inch teeth do exist and their authenticity has been established. Therefore, *C. megalodon* was certainly much larger than scientists previously suspected.

It might be interesting to hypothesize the plausible size of this giant if a pair of jaws were to be reconstructed using the *newly* discovered eight-inch teeth. The construction of these jaws could indeed promise a model much larger than the restoration made years ago by the American Museum of Natural History. Comparatively speaking, it could be assumed that the giant might have attained a length of at least 120 feet!

It is difficult to comprehend the apparent immensity of this prehistoric colossus. By way of illustration, a comparison with a large object,

A scale drawing illustrating the hypothetical enormity of Carcharodon megalodon. *Based upon the most recent fossil teeth discoveries, it may have measured as much as 120 feet. I have compared its length of 120 feet with the average 45-foot trailer truck. This gigantean creature terrorized the Miocene seas but reached an evolutionary cul-de-sac 12 million years ago. Its evolvement and extinction still remain a mystery.*

one that we are all familiar with, would make this profound analogy easier. For example, take the large trailer trucks we often see on our cross-country highways. These huge trucks are some of our largest road vehicles and average 45 feet in length. When comparing one of these

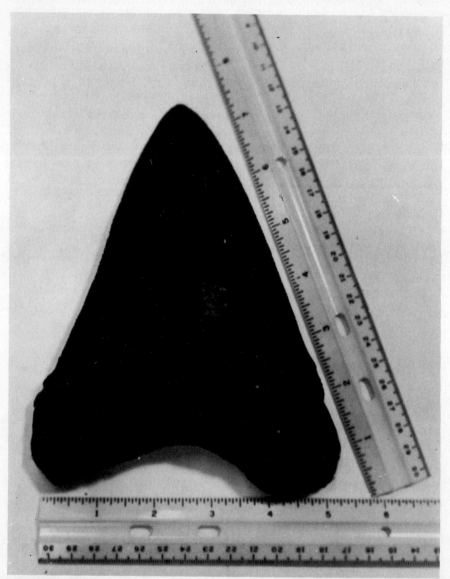

A plaster cast of Carcharodon megalodon's *fossil tooth that would have measured eight inches if time had not eroded and reduced its true size. Larger teeth have been discovered recently, but their authenticity has not yet been established. (Courtesy Bone Valley Museum, Bradley, Florida)*

trucks against a hypothetical profile of *C. megalodon*, the truck would
be about one-third as long as the shark. In fact, *C. megalodon* could
almost engulf the entire truck within its gigantic jaws!

Until now, the blue whale had been considered the largest creature
that ever existed. (A record specimen measured 113½ feet and its
weight was estimated at 170 tons). With the recent discovery of *C.
megalodon's* large teeth, however, it is now feasible to presume that
C. megalodon was larger than the blue whale. It would be difficult to
estimate its weight, but, a figure well over 200 tons might be within
the realm of possibility!

An aura of mystery surrounds *C. megalodon*, and many questions
concerning its existence and dimensions are still unanswered. Its sudden appearance in the Miocene epoch and its disappearance after a
comparatively short span of time (while its close relatives continued
to flourish) leave the scientists puzzled. Was the emergence of this
particular giant species one of nature's strange whims? Did she then
decide that this creature didn't fit into her plan and forced it to become extinct? Or did she reduce its size to that of *C. carcharias*, our
present-day great white shark? There are many theories but no indis-
putable facts, therefore, some paleontologists believe that during the
reign of *C. megalodon*, the great white shark, *C. carcharias*, also existed as *C. sulcidens* whose teeth are similar to those of our modern
great white. These mysterious forms of evolution are called "diverg-
ence and parallelism of the species" and are often found in other
species among the many vertebrates.

Present-day writings do not offer any simple concept of *C. megalodon's* evolvement and extinction. Records do not suggest any kind of
theory or supposition as to why nature suddenly created this incredible
giant, thrust it among its relatives that had successfully existed for over
300 million years, and then caused its extinction after the comparatively short reign of only 16 million years.

Unfortunately, we have no detailed description or other evidence of
its size except estimates made from its huge fossil teeth. Like its close
relatives, it was a vertebrate possessing a cartilaginous structure that
deteriorated rapidly, making it a poor object for fossilization. Ironically, we have a well-rounded picture of the ancient reptile family that
existed more than 50 million years *prior* to *C. megalodon*. They, however, were vertebrates whose hard bony skeletons were preserved for
eons in sedimentary formations.

In spite of all our speculating, two burning questions still remain:
Why did this great creature, which evolved from hardy and enduring
stock, suddenly leave its position of complete supremacy in the sea?
Why did its smaller relatives continue to thrive and develop (under
similar environmental conditions) into modern sharks as we know
them today? It is a puzzle that defies solution. The few clues, the

If Carcharodon had *existed during the Mesozoic era, this dramatic scene could have taken place. However, according to fossil records,* Carcharodon *mysteriously appeared approximately 80 million years later during the Miocene epoch and only its smaller ancestors existed during the reign of* Tyrannosaurus rex.

fossilized remains, offer little help. In spite of this apparent impasse, the immensity of *C. megalodon* must certainly excite the curiosity of both scientists and laymen and we may yet discover the cause of its extinction. As man continues to explore his planet, perhaps one day, somewhere, an answer will be found in the stratified rock formations or from some other yet-untapped source.

The miraculous story of life is revealed in the rocks of the earth. Like a huge book, the many layers of rock unfold the story of the earth's past, chapter by chapter. In learning to read this story of prehistoric life, man has had to understand these rock formations and be able to identify the many fossils they contain. Some fossils are found along the seashores; some upon the open plains; others on the floor of vanished oceans. They are found wherever sands have been compressed into rock.

The word *fossil* stems from the Latin word *fossilis,* which is derived from the verb root *fodere* meaning *to dig.* Fossils play an important part in interpreting the earth's past history and the environmental changes that have taken place during its many geological eras. Scientists are able to determine the approximate age of fossils or prehistoric organic residue by a method of radiocarbon dating.

There are still many puzzles and "missing links" concerning prehistoric life that remain unsolved today. Only paleontologists with specialized knowledge of geology and biology can understand the many intricate and delicate procedures involved in identifying, classifying, and restoring a freshly unearthed fossil.

A special kind of excitement occurs when someone discovers a prehistoric shark tooth along a remote coastal beach or in an inland fossil deposit. It stems from the knowledge that this particular tooth is all that remains of a primitive creature belonging to an extinct species of fish.

Fossil collecting can become contagious and often becomes a serious hobby. It offers a special front seat for reviewing the past to anyone who has the faintest glimmer of interest in the present world of living things. It is educational, satisfying, and remarkable, too, since it deals with some of the oldest creatures and plants preserved (just as they looked) when they were caught in their rocky "prisons." Collecting and studying fossils gives us a better understanding of prehistory and also the feeling that we are actually linked with the past. We get a better feeling for prehistory when we are able to see and handle fossils instead of merely reading words and looking at pictures. We seem to form a closer association with nature and develop more interest and appreciation for our own environment.

Those who wish to pursue the study of fossil sharks should acquire a copy of *Fossil Sharks and Fish Remains of North America* by Gerard R. Case (1967). Mr. Case's book is well written and illustrated profusely, in keeping with his reputation as one of America's well-known amateur paleontologists. It can be used as a guide to the identification of fossils, offering many collecting techniques, and suggesting many fertile localities for finding specimens. Case has written another book called *Fossils Illustrated* (1968), an excellent guide for amateur and professional paleontologists. Each book can be obtained by writing to Gerard R. Case, 225 St. Paul's Avenue, Jersey City, New Jersey, 07306.

2
Spectres of the Present

OF THE MORE THAN 250 CLASSIFIED SPECIES OF SHARKS FOUND THROUGH-out the world, over half are considered rare. Among the remaining species (except for slight differences in anatomy) are many that are classified as separate species regardless of their similarity. It would be impossible to catalogue all species, since their identities would overlap. For these reasons I have listed only those common sharks that fall into the following categories: biological oddities, menaces to man's survival, laboratory creatures used in medical research, game for sportfishing, and objects of commercial usage.

Since the nature of this text is nonscientific, I have made no attempt to use complete taxonomic nomenclature in identifying sharks and related species. Only their common names, genera, and species are given. However, the accompanying drawings were prepared with care so that the reader can refer to them for identification purposes.

BASKING SHARK
(Cetorhinus maximus)

Although the basking shark is not related to the whale shark in any way, it is the second largest living fish known to man. These creatures can reach 45 feet in length and weigh several tons. Their colors range from slate gray to grayish brown, while their undersides are slightly lighter with a prominent white triangular patch under the snout.

Basking sharks possess extremely long gill openings with matching gill rakers (cartilaginous protrusions inside the gill arch) which, when used like sieves, trap plankton and small fish from the water. They are slow, harmless creatures, long in body with elongated, pointed snouts and mouths that contain numerous minute teeth.

Normally a cold-water species, the basking shark seldom appears anywhere in the tropical waters of the world but has a large range of distribution throughout the temperate zones both above and below the equator.

Basking sharks are caught commercially for their oil by harpooning methods in Irish and Scottish waters where small fisheries exist. They are strong swimmers and often dive several hundred feet to the bottom, burying themselves in the mud in an effort to free themselves of the harpoons.

BLUE SHARK
(Prionace glauca)

The blue shark is handsome in appearance and is distinguished by its brilliant blue back and snow-white belly. Apart from its color, the chief anatomical characteristics that distinguish it from other sharks are its extremely slender body with a pointed snout and its long, narrow pectoral fins.

Often called the great blue shark, it attains a length of 15 feet with isolated cases reported up to 20 feet. Because of its elongated body, a blue shark will weigh much less compared to other sharks of a similar length. A blue weighing 250 pounds will sometimes measure only 11 or 12 feet.

Blue sharks have a fairly wide range of distribution. They are strictly oceanic in character, roaming about with other pelagic sharks, but sometimes they venture into inshore waters in search of food. There are large populations of blue sharks located along the entire west coast and the northeast coast of the United States.

Heavy concentraions of blue sharks are also found in Irish waters, the southwest coast of England, and the west coast of Africa. According to surveys made by the U.S. Fish and Wildlife Service, the blue shark may be the most prolific of all the pelagic sharks in the Atlantic and Pacific oceans.

The largest blue shark listed in the I.G.F.A. records weighed 410 pounds and was caught in 1960 on 80-pound test line off Rockport, Massachusetts, by Dr. Richard C. Webster. Seven years later, his daughter Martha evened the score by catching a blue that weighed exactly the same on the same test line and even in the same waters. Both anglers are listed, tied, in the I.G.F.A. all-tackle record book!

BROWN SHARK
(*Carcharhinus milberti*)

The brown shark (often called sandbar shark) is the shark most frequently reported, inhabiting the coastal waters of the western Atlantic from New York to southern Florida. It is found in fewer numbers in the Gulf of Mexico and off the coast of southern Brazil.

The most distinctive characteristic of the brown shark is its large first dorsal fin, the height of which exceeds 10 percent of its entire length; also, its position is further forward (in relation to the pectoral fins) than any other species.

As its name implies, it is grayish brown in color with a dirty white belly. Brown sharks reach up to eight feet in length and seldom weigh more than 250 pounds.

An angler would rate the brown shark only average as far as game characterists are concerned. Taken on light tackle the brown will offer a fair scrap.

Although brown sharks have often attacked a fairly large hooked fish, they are not considered a threat to swimmers.

BULL SHARK
(*Carcharhinus leucas*)

The bull shark is an easy species to identify since it has a snout that is broadly rounded and short when compared to other sharks. In addition, its first dorsal fin is located farther forward (in relation to its pectoral fins) than most other species. Because of this most taxidermists, when making a head mount, include the dorsal fin as well as the usual pectoral fin.

The bull (also known as the cub shark) is a heavy-bodied animal and, when fully mature, reaches 12 feet in length and weighs as much as 500 pounds or more.

It has a white belly, with pale gray sides blending into a dark gray shade on top. The tips of the fins are dark in young sharks while the pectoral fins will be tipped with a dusky color in the mature ones.

This is a slow-swimming species except when it is disturbed or excited by the presence of food or while it is fighting a rod and reel. From the viewpoint of the angler, the bull puts up a good, short fight. However, toward the end it loses its spirit and is whipped into submission with little effort.

The bull shark has a large area of distribution and is found primarily in the inshore waters of the temperate and warm seas of the western Atlantic Ocean from New York to southern Brazil, around Bermuda, the West Indies, in Lakes Nicaragua and Yzabal, and in Central American tributaries. Here, it is known as the Lake Nicaragua shark (*Carcharhinus nicaraguensis*) and is able to exist in both fresh and salt water.

Another close relative and a fresh-water variant of the bull shark is the South Africa Zambezi shark (*Carcharhinus zambezensis*) found along that coast and as far as 200 miles upriver from the ocean.

COMMON HAMMERHEAD SHARK
(*Sphyrna zygaena*)

The bizarre shape of the head of the hammerhead is different from that of any other shark. This weird creature is easy to identify even at a distance because of its unusual appearance. As the name implies, its head is shaped somewhat like a hammer; that is, there are two projecting appendages, one on each side, and at the extreme end of each appendage is an eye that seems capable of rotating like a ball bearing. Ichthyologists find the creature exceptionally interesting. Some speculate that nature must be experimenting with this strange hydrodynamic shape that might serve as a horizontal steering device, allowing the shark to maneuver more effectively and increasing its area of vision.

Seven species make up this family, and positive identification of each is usually made from the slight variations in the shape and structure of the head. The great hammerhead (*Sphyrna mokarran*) is the largest of the species and has been known to reach 18 feet in length and up to 1500 pounds in weight. The smallest of the species is the bonnethead shark (*Sphyrna tiburo*), which is often called the shovelnose or shovelhead shark. The width of the head is much shorter in the bonnethead than in the other species, but anglers still confuse the two. Bonnetheads average about three feet in length and are inhabitants of shallow water. Small bonnetheads are often caught by bone fishermen cruising the flats.

Coloration in the whole hammerhead family is quite similar. They have brown or ash grey backs and sides, and all have creamy-white bellies. They have rather small mouths in comparison with other sharks, but their dorsal fins are much larger.

The range of distribution of the hammerheads will vary. All species inhabit the tropical or temperate zones of the oceans, but some are able to tolerate cooler water than others. Hammerheads are commonly seen at the surface in both inshore and offshore waters and frequently pursue small fish that inhabit the shallows.

The liver is large and the oil derived from it is rich in vitamin A. But the hammerhead is one of the few sharks whose hide is undesirable for the manufacture of leather products.

The U.S. Navy considers the hammerhead very dangerous and a potential threat to swimmers. It has the maximum rating of four plus (4+) and is in the same category as the great white shark and the mako. Official records disclose that there have been numerous attacks made upon swimmers. Human remains have been discovered in the stomachs of many hammerheads.

The hammerhead is a powerful swimmer and a hardy fighter. Avid anglers always appreciate the seemingly unlimited endurance qualities of the critter. It will often ignore a dead bait and then readily take a live one such as a jack or a snapper.

GREAT WHITE SHARK
(Carcharodon carcharias)

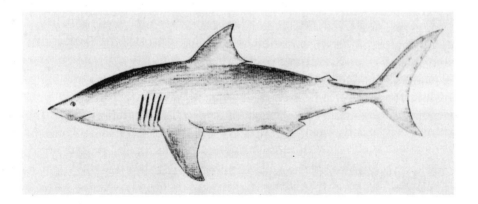

This is the man-eater that any red-blooded "sharker" would be proud to latch onto and complain about sore muscles for later. With the exception of the killer whale (Orca), whose bad reputation borders on the legendary, the great white (for its size) is the most vicious creature in the ocean. Except for the lumbering whale shark and sleepy basking shark that are quite harmless, it is the giant of present-

day game species. Official estimates indicate that it can reach a weight
of 8,000 pounds and measure well over 30 feet in length. One that
weighed 7,302 pounds and measured 21 feet was caught in Cuban
waters during the mid-forties.

The great white is a direct descendant of the extinct, prehistoric
Carcharodon megalodon that roamed the seas 20 million years ago
during the Miocene era. Countless fossilized teeth of this species have
been found, and some measure more than seven inches in length!

Our present-day great white shark is a formidable killer. This mean
and always hungry shark seldom refuses a baited hook or even an
artificially rigged lure. It is readily accepted by anglers throughout the
world as a great game fish. Alfred Dean of Ceduna, South Australia,
caught a world-record white shark in 1959 on 130-pound test line. It
weighed 2,664 pounds and measured 16 feet, 10 inches. This is still
the official International Game Fish Association record.

Although whites are being caught with some regularity along both
coasts of North Central and South America, they are more prevalent
in the coastal waters of Australia and New Zealand. Rod-and-reel
catches frequently exceed 1,000 pounds. Sharks weighing 3,000 and
4,000 pounds have frequently been caught on commercial longlines,
in nets, or with harpoons, but it takes a special breed of angler to
roam the seas in search of a great white and then spend the many
grueling hours necessary to subdue the beast while using what most
people consider flimsy, delicate, or inappropriate equipment.

The white shark is a pelagic species that inhabits the open waters
of both the tropical and temperate zones. It is commonly found along
the coasts of southeastern Australia, but there are occasions when this
marauder will leave its offshore environment and cruise the reefs and
shallows in search of food.

Whenever a great white is caught and dissected, an examination of
its stomach contents is enough to stun the imagination! All sorts of
creatures have been found: seals, turtles, squids, rays, sea lions, dogs,
porpoises, and other sharks some of which weighed more than 100
pounds! Apparently their appetites are insatiable, since some stomachs
also contain such refuse as auto tires, boat planks (many reports verify
unprovoked attacks upon boats), cans, whiskey bottles, light bulbs,
oil drums, books, and garbage.

But the real horror that surrounds the great white comes from its
reputation as a killer of people. Hence its alias "man-eater." According
to official records, the man-eater is directly responsible for many
attacks upon bathers, skin divers, downed flyers, and shipwrecked
sailors. A few attacks were provoked but many were not, and few
victims were left alive to relate their nightmarish experiences. Also
called the "white death," this villain is considered the most dangerous
and ferocious species in the entire shark family and is responsible for

the majority of the unprovoked and fatal attacks on record.

The great white is heavy bodied with a streamlined shape and a pointed snout (often called "whitepointer" in Australia). Its caudal fin or tail section closely resembles that of a fish but the dorsal lobe is slightly longer than the lower lobe. There is a keel located at the caudal peduncle, which is usually found only in the swift-moving fishes such as in the tuna and billfish families. No doubt nature intended this small projection to serve as a stabilizing aid to increase its speed and maneuverability. They have even been seen jumping and leaping over the water while pursuing a school of fish.

Contrary to its name, the color of the great white is not really white except for the underside, which is off-white—a characteristic found in most ocean-roaming sharks. The rest of the body varies from blue-gray to an almost black while larger species are slate gray.

LEMON SHARK
(*Negaprion brevirostris*)

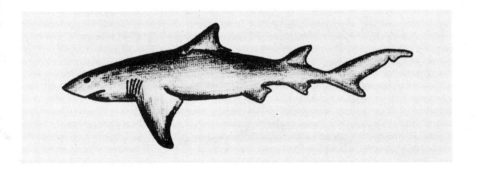

Lemon sharks are widely distributed throughout the tropical and subtropical oceans of the world. However, they rarely inhabit deep water, and are usually found in the various inshore reefs, shallow flats, bays, and the mouths of rivers. Some species have an unusual tolerance for sweet water and have been caught in the brackish waters of tidal estuaries miles away from the ocean.

Lemon sharks are yellowish-brown on their backs and sides, gradually fusing into a yellowish-white belly. Immature lemons are lighter in color but they darken with maturity.

It is easy to recognize the lemon shark by the similarity in the size and shape of its two dorsal fins. Sand sharks (*Carcharias taurus*) share this same anatomical characteristic but are distinquished from the lemons by their pointed snouts and the shape and position of their anal fins. The snout of the lemon is blunt and broadly rounded when viewed from above. It has small, catlike eyes that have a tinge of yellow-green color. Its teeth are very sharp, slightly curved, and symmetrical, with no cusps at the margins.

Lemon sharks that are commonly caught weigh from 150 to 250 pounds and at this weight are approximately eight feet in length with a proportionately large girth. Those of 300 pounds are quite rare, although there is one record of a 400-pound lemon that measured 11 feet.

Lemon sharks are excellent subjects for the laboratory and, with proper care, soon become acclimated to captivity and continue to flourish for long periods of time. A good number of lemons are used for demonstrations and observation because they tolerate frequent handling and anesthesia. They are also popular in aquarium exhibits and have been known to thrive for as long as five years. As a rule, they are sensitive to any severe change in water temperature. When a captive lemon experiences a sudden drop in water temperature, it usually responds poorly to experiments and will often refuse food until the temperature is brought back to a more comfortable level.

MAKO SHARK
(*Isurus oxyrinchus*) , (*Isurus glaucus*)

Bearing a physical resemblance to the white shark, the Atlantic (*Isurus oxyrinchus*) and Pacific makos (*Isurus glaucus*), sometimes called the bonito shark, also pursue a similar course of assault and destruction. They are gracefully streamlined, and their similarity to the great white is noted in their lunate, fishlike tails and pointed snouts. Although the average mako does not attain the large dimension of the white, what the mako lacks in size it makes up in speed, and it shares the same degree of aggressiveness and voraciousness.

The mako is a pelagic or open-ocean wanderer that ventures occasionally into inshore waters. Its distribution is similar to the white shark's in that both are found in warm temperate and tropical seas. It is a handsome shark: well-proportioned, streamlined, and colored a striking blue-gray on top with an almost snow-white underside.

In some areas the mako shark is called a "sharp-nosed mackerel" and in some restaurants it is called "swordfish"! The flesh is so similar in taste and appearance that only the most discriminating gourmet can detect the difference! Actually, the meat of the mako shark is considered the finest tasting of all sharks, and at times, in some coastal areas, the demand is greater than the supply. Although most people shudder at the thought of eating a shark, if we call it "swordfish" the magic word erases all unpleasant thoughts from the mind of the diner.

Because of the mako's speed (clocked at more than 30 knots), it is able to pursue and feed upon school fish such as the tuna, mackerel, and some members of the herring family. Some marine scientists believe that the extra tasty flavor of mako is a result of its diet of fast-moving fish. This is probably speculation since the flesh of many slow-moving sharks is also considered very tasty, and they are scavenger-like feeders eating only a wide variety of bottom creatures.

The Atlantic and Pacific makos share the same fighting qualities that deep-sea anglers genuinely respect. Judged to be the swiftest of all the sharks, they are better known for their acrobatic capers when hooked. The fight with rod and reel is spectacular. Their runs are long and strong and they offer little quarter to the angler. They are dangerous to bring to gaff for they make fantastic leaps and, sometimes, when enraged, they will deliberately attack the boat. The makos, along with the white sharks, are classified as man-eaters and records reveal that they, too, are responsible for a number of attacks on men and boats. They are rated 4+ by the U.S. Navy as a maximum danger potential to swimmers.

The feeding habits of the mako are unusual. In addition to pursuing schools of tuna, mackerel, and herring, they have a strange affinity for the flesh of the broadbill swordfish. The swordfish is considered one of the finest, most courageous game fish in the sea, yet anglers who hook swordfish are always afraid that a mako might attack their prize. The mako's appetite is insatiable and it exhibits no fear of man nor fish. It is nothing for a 200-pound mako to gouge out a 50-pound chunk of flesh from a 500-pound swordfish! In 1939 Michael Lerner, founder of the International Game Fish Association, caught a 720-pound mako whose stomach contained a 110-pound swordfish intact except for the tail section. The mako and the swordfish are apparently mortal enemies as they have been sighted in furious battles during the spring in the straits of Florida.

The average mako will measure six feet in length and weigh approximately 150 pounds, but they have been caught up to 13 feet in length and weighing well over 1,000 pounds. The official records of the International Game Fish Association show that the largest mako caught on rod and reel weighed 1,061 pounds. It was caught by James Penwarden in 1970 on 130-pound line in New Zealand waters.

Like most other big game fish, the mako will strike a trolled bait or artificial lure such as a hook-rigged Hawaiian teaser or a large top feather. Most of the time they are not fussy about taking a bait because their appetite overcomes any natural cautious instincts they may possess. Makos can also be caught by drifting a dead or live bait in a chum line of ground fish and blood.

NURSE SHARK
(*Ginglymostoma cirratum*)

Although there is no similarity between the nurse shark and the dreaded Australian grey nurse (*Carcharias arenarius*), modern literature makes no explanation for the origin of its name. The nurse shark is an ungainly, ponderous-looking creature; nothing about it creates the impression of sleek and formidable terror usually ascociated with other sharks.

It is dark brownish-yellow in color on its back and sides, gradually changing to a yellow ochre on the underbelly. The color in immature species is almost identical except that they are covered with small black spots.

Nurse sharks have unusually small eyes and exceptionally large nostrils. Biologists believe that they depend almost completely upon their olfactory senses when searching for food rather than upon their lateris system, which receives vibrations from a live food source. A pair of fleshy appendages (called barbels) are located adjacent to their nostrils. These serve as their sensorial touch organs. This equipment is similar in function to that of catfish, which also possess small barbels located on the lower lip.

Although the mouth and many cusped teeth of the nurse shark are smaller in comparison to other sharks, its jaws are strong and are used mainly for crushing rather than ripping or tearing. Obviously, nature intended this bottom dweller to feed upon crustacea, shellfish, and other creatures such as the spiny boxfish, cowfish, and trunkfish.

Except for slight variations, the pectoral fins of most sharks are situated in a ventral (almost vertical) position. In the nurse shark, however, the shoulder girdle fixes the pectoral fin in a lateral or nearly horizontal position. This allows it to glide along the bottom in a more raylike fashion than other sharks, which can execute swift or acute maneuvers. They have often been observed using their large pectoral fins to secure a better position under rocks and crevices. When we consider their locomotion, habitat, appearance, and disposition, this species suggests a closer link to the rays than to the family of sharks!

Nurse sharks have a small range of distribution and are confined to the more tropical waters. They inhabit the shallow waters of the tropical Atlantic and the Pacific Coast from the Gulf of California down to Ecuador.

Unlike the skin of most other sharks, the skin of the nurse is smooth, thick, and tough—with an extra layer of gristlelike material supporting the skin. It is popular with manufacturers of leather products, and tanneries pay premium prices to the commercial shark fishermen who can furnish them with satisfactory hides.

Nurse sharks are rugged creatures and require little oxygen. Unlike most of the other sharks that are forced to keep moving in order to absorb enough oxygen from the water moving through their gills, nurses can lie motionless on the bottom for great lengths of time without ill effects. Because of this factor and their docile disposition, they are ideal creatures for captivity and make excellent laboratory subjects because they require little attention. They are also popular in public aquariums and, in one instance, a nurse shark has been kept alive in captivity for the past 25 years.

PORBEAGLE SHARK
(*Lamna nasus*)

Together with the mako shark, the porbeagle is often referred to in literature as the mackerel shark. Apparently, this name confusion stems from the shark's eating habits, since the porbeagle also feeds heavily upon the school mackerel, herring, and other similar swift-moving fish. The porbeagle does bear an anatomical resemblance to the great white and the mako, although it never attains the enormous size of its cousins. They all have fishlike tails, but the porbeagle has two keels on the caudal fin. From its appearance the porbeagle might be expected to assume the role of a formidable, sea-going terror. However, on rod and reel the porbeagle offers little of the fighting qualities exhibited by its cousins but it is a fast-swimming creature and can give the angler some interesting action.

Shark-attack records reveal no porbeagle assaults upon man or boat. However, sometime, the porbeagle surely will be implicated in an attack on man. And why not? He has equipment similar to all dangerous sharks and all sharks are unpredictable. This makes the porbeagle a potential threat to man; so it is rated 2+ by the U.S. Naval Department as a possible danger to swimmers, especially when provoked.

The porbeagle prefers cooler water than its relatives and can be found in the continental waters of the northern Atlantic, northern Pacific, Australia, and New Zealand. It is bluish gray on top and near white on the belly.

The food value of the porbeagle is apparently very good since a popular demand exists for it in Europe. The flavor is known to resemble that of the swordfish. According to United Nations statistics, the porbeagle shark must be extremely popular in Italy because over a million pounds a year are shipped to that country from the Scandinavian countries. The Germans also favor the porbeagle flesh, and the price it brings at the market is sometimes almost four times that of the cod.

The porbeagle shark has been known to reach a length of 10 feet, but most specimens caught on hook and line are much smaller. The International Game Fish Association lists one catch of 430 pounds that was taken off the English coast on 80-pound test line.

The Pacific porbeagle, also called the salmon shark (*Lamna ditropus*), is almost identical to the Atlantic porbeagle, also prefers cooler water, and is found in both the open sea and coastal waters. Enthusiastic West Coast anglers use salmon for bait while the Easterners have their best success with mackerel, squid, or cod.

SAND SHARK
(*Carcharias taurus*)

Sand sharks (also called sand tigers) share similar dorsal fins with lemon sharks. However, the sand shark has a more pointed snout and its teeth are ragged and spike shaped. Coloration is gray-brown on top and the belly is grayish white. Some specimens are mottled with irregular dark markings that cover the posterior section of the trunk and part of the tail.

Sand sharks exceed 10 feet in length and weigh as much as 400 pounds. A mediocre fighter by anglers' standards, it exhibits little endurance and is quickly whipped into submission.

Its area of distribution is almost worldwide, ranging from the Indo-Pacific, Mediterranean, tropical West Africa, South Africa, Gulf of Maine to Florida, Brazil, and Argentina.

Sand sharks constitute a dangerous threat to swimmers and are rated 2+ by the U.S. Navy since they have been implicated in attacks upon people and boats. Their close relative, the formidable gray nurse shark (*Carcharias arenarius*) of Australia also has a sinister reputation and is responsible for a number of attacks upon swimmers.

SMALL BLACK-TIPPED SHARK
(*Carcharhinus limbatus*)

The small and large black-tipped sharks are frequently called spinners or black-tip spinners because of the peculiar way they leap from the water and spiral in the air. They are streamlined, well-proportioned sharks colored blue-grey or bronze-grey on their tops and sides, shading from white to a yellowish-white on their bellies. Their name is derived from the prominent black patches on the tips of their fins.

Small black-tipped sharks are pelagic and are found in most of the tropical and subtropical waters of the Atlantic and Pacific oceans. There seems to be an unusually heavy concentration of small black-tipped sharks in the Caribbean and south Florida waters during the spring and fall when they move in close to shore. Literature cites several other species of small and large black-tipped sharks in this group but positive identification is obscure and sometimes even contradictory.

The small black-tipped shark is often confused with its close relative (large black-tipped shark) because its anatomical characteristics and color are the same. The small black-tipped shark has smaller gill slits, larger eyes, and its dorsal fin is located closer to the head. The large black-tipped shark *is* larger, although literature is vague as to exactly what size the species attains and what range of distribution it has.

The small black-tipped shark is an active, vigorous species, forever on the prowl for food. They often inhabit inshore waters, bays, river mouths, and beach areas where they are seen frequently by swimmers and caught in quantity by anglers. They must have some tolerance for fresh water, for they have been found in brackish water well up into the estuarine areas where the salt water joints the sweet.

THRESHER SHARK
(*Alopias vulpinus*)

The unusual tail, almost as long as its body, distinguishes the thresher shark from any other member of the shark clan. Its name originated from the peculiar habit of this creature of flailing (or threshing) a school of smaller fish or any other unsuspecting quarry with its huge, formidable tail.

Commercial net fishermen first observed that thresher sharks have the ability to surround and "run herd" on schools of mackerel or menhaden. After the school fish were herded and packed into a tight mass, the threshers would suddenly bore in, slam the small fish mercilessly with their strong sicklelike tails, and then turn swiftly about to gulp down the floundering victims. Apparently, the thresher's real fighting talent lies in the power and agility of this extremely long appendage rather than in its teeth. The thresher's mouth is small and weak in structure, but it more than makes up for this lack with the use of its tail.

Coloration varies in the different species and ranges from blue-grey to brown and sometimes black on the back and sides. Some species have a mottled appearance but all of them have a white belly. All species of this genus have fairly large eyes, but there is one species rarely caught called the "big-eyed thresher" because of its unusually large eyes. Ichthyologists presume this species inhabits exceptionally deep water.

Compared to other sharks, there is very little information available on the thresher, probably because of its scarcity and wide distribution. They are known to reach a length of 18 to 20 feet and weigh in excess of 1,000 pounds, but these large specimens are seldom caught.

Threshers are pelagic and inhabit the tropical and temperate zones of all oceans. They are known to venture occasionally into the inshore waters in search of school fish. They seem to be quite prolific along the coasts of New South Wales, Australia, New Zealand, and California. Anglers in these areas catch them regularly. The fighting qualities of the thresher are only moderate although it is a strong swimmer—probably due to the power of its large tail.

Official shark-attack records indicate that the threshers have not been implicated in any attacks upon people. However, records show that there have been two attacks upon boats. On the other hand, it has been reported by observers that threshers have been seen acting very timidly and, in fact, deliberately avoiding any contact with boats!

The I.G.F.A. lists an all-tackle record thresher that weighed 922 pounds. No one has been able to better this catch that was landed by W. W. Dowding on 130-pound line off the Bay of Islands, New Zealand, in 1937.

TIGER SHARK
(Galeocerdo cuvieri)

The tiger shark (alias the leopard shark) was named for its tiger-like markings. These conspicuous oblique stripes and patches gradually disappear as it reaches maturity in its seventh or eighth year. Its growth rate is quite rapid, averaging about 12 inches each year until the tenth or eleventh year when the growing process begins to slow down. Tigers of 10 or 12 feet are commonly caught by commercial and sports fishermen. The largest tiger sharks in the world are said to inhabit the Indian Ocean; they have been reported to measure 25 to 30 feet in length and weigh in excess of 2,500 pounds.

The tiger has large, round eyes and a short snout that is wide and rounded when viewed from above. Its teeth are small compared to other sharks of similar size and weight, but they are thick and wide with a notch at the inner margin. All the edges are serrated and when it bites an object, the result is a clean and efficient cut.

Tiger sharks seem to be flexible creatures and have a great range of distribution. They are found in all tropical and subtropical oceans of the world, although they appear to be more common in the tropics and near oceanic islands. So far, no clearly defined migratory pattern has been established except in a few areas such as central Florida's east coast, where they are found in abundance during the fall and off South Carolina in the summer. Tigers frequent both inshore and offshore waters in their relentless search for food.

Knowledge of the breeding habits of these creatures is vague, although there is some conjecture that the gravid female tiger will seek inshore or shallow water to give birth to its young. It has been reported that large females are capable of bearing more than 100 young in a single litter!

Tiger sharks have always been popular at marine exhibitions because of their size and formidable appearance. Spectators stand in awe and shudder when one of these frightening, yet graceful, man-eaters swims close to the sight-seeing windows separating man from beast by only a few inches. Tigers are also popular because they are able to adapt fairly well to captivity. Their tolerance depends mostly upon their physical condition before entering the holding tanks. Like most sharks, some go into shock, refuse to eat, or die of internal injuries possibly received during the capturing operation. Strict policing is necessary to prevent cannibalism, one of the tiger's better-known characteristics.

Frequently, commercial shark fishermen concentrate on tiger sharks just for the hides. After the denticles have been removed at the tannery, the hide (which is considerably stronger than most other sharks' or animals') discloses an exceptionally attractive grain. Leading manufacturers of leather goods consider the tiger shark hide excellent for fine quality shoes, wallets, belts, etc.

Most tiger sharks appear sluggish in their movements and exhibit an air of detachment to their surroundings. When they are in pursuit of food or come in contact with an angler's hook, however, all of these characteristics vanish immediately. They become powerful, greedy critters that offer extreme resistance to being captured. Fishing for the tiger is an excellent sport, and is most desired by many shark anglers. According to the I.G.F.A., the all-tackle record for this shark is a 1,780-pounder caught by Walter Maxwell on 130-pound test line off Cherry Grove, South Carolina, in 1964.

The U.S. Navy rates the tiger shark two plus (2+) a higher rating than many other sharks suspected of being dangerous. It is responsible for numerous unprovoked attacks upon people and boats all over the world. The tiger is especially feared by people because it is likely to venture close to shore, into river mouths, and well up into the estuaries. Apparently it has a reasonable tolerance for surviving in brackish water.

It is common knowledge that extremely large tiger sharks roam the waters along the coastlines bordering the Indian Ocean. Many attacks recorded in these areas named the tiger as the villain. In addition, numerous natives, sailors, divers, and fishermen have disappeared in these same areas. The "tiger of the sea" could have taken any number of these victims without anyone's knowledge of the tragedy. Recorders of official shark attacks suspect regretfully that their existing journals could be supplemented considerably if only the real truth about these missing people were known.

WHALE SHARK
(*Rhincodon typus*)

Although it is completely unrelated to the whale except in size, the whale shark is the largest of the clan and one of the most docile. Its color is dark grey-green, marked conspicuously with almost white spots. Its monstrous size and color pattern make it unique and easy to identify. It has a huge mouth, almost as broad as its head, with numerous minute teeth which, in cooperation with its interconnected gill equipment, are able to strain plankton and small fish from the water.

The whale shark is a slow, lumbering creature that averages 30 feet in length but reports made by observers claim that it can reach 60 feet in length. A 38-foot specimen was captured off the Florida Keys in 1912. The monster, weighing over 26,000 pounds, was preserved and exhibited throughout the South from a railroad flatcar.

With a great range of distribution, the whale shark is found in all the tropical oceans and has been sighted as far north as New York and, in the Pacific, as far as Japan. It inhabits offshore waters and is known as the largest living fish.

Since the whale shark feeds exclusively upon small marine organisms, it poses no threat to man except that, when molested, its great tail can capsize a small boat.

WHITETIP OCEANIC SHARK
(*Carcharhinus longimanus*)

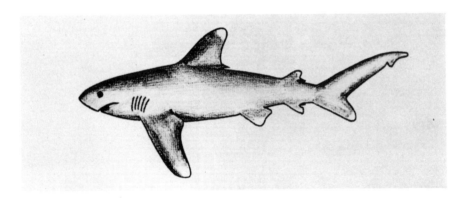

The whitetip oceanic shark receives its name from its distinctive white-tipped fins and caudal lobes. The first dorsal fin is broadly rounded and the rear tip of the anal fin almost reaches the lower caudal lobe of the tail. The body color varies from bluish gray to pale brown above and a yellowish dirty white below.

These are deep-water sharks and are thought to be the most abundant warm-water pelagic species, usually encountered in water that exceeds 100 fathoms and seldom found in inshore waters. They are widely distributed in tropical and warm temperate areas of the Pacific, Atlantic, and Indian Oceans.

Adult whitetips reach 12 feet in length and are judged to be very dangerous, having been implicated in many attacks upon air and sea disaster survivors.

Little is known about these sharks since they are out of range of most anglers. However, repellent tests made upon this species had negative results.

Whitetip oceanic sharks are closely related to the whitetip reef sharks (*Carcharhinus albimarginatus*) that are considerably smaller (up to eight feet in length) but possess similar anatomical features. These are frequently found in the warm seas around reefs and coral atolls and are believed to be dangerous.

3

A Biological Sea-going Engine

SHARKS HAVE EXISTED LONGER THAN MOST PRESENT-DAY CREATURES. EX-cept for that huge prehistoric bruiser the great white shark (*Carcharo-don megalodon*), whose length has been estimated at over 80 feet, sharks have remained essentially unchanged in both structure and function while many other sea and land animals became extinct as they made their way up that long and precarious ladder of evolution. Sharks have survived because they possessed the unique ability to adapt to their slow but ever-changing environment. This alone marks them as a biological phenomenon. They are exceptionally hardy and almost impervious to disease. From all indications, they are going to be with us still unchanged for many millions of years.

I like to think of the shark as a powerful, rugged, and efficient machine that requires little fuel and never breaks down. The shark has often been called "a perfect biological sea-going engine," and I feel that the description is very accurate. If we take this unique engine apart and examine its wonderous machinery we cannot help admiring the manner in which it operates or the architect who designed it.

Biologically speaking, this robust creature is an important benefactor to man in several ways. Its structure and organs are particularly important to scientific researchers who realize that the shark's organs have been instrumental in solving various medical problems related to human physiology, immunology, and virology. Some of their organs are complex in structure; others are relatively simple, but all are totally efficient and practically free of disease or disorder.

For example, consider the liver, whose fats contain a sophisticated defense substance. This material contains antibodies that have the ability to combat disease-producing viruses that invade the shark's body. Lipid, a fatlike substance that is normally found in all animals, was discovered in large, potent quantities in the shark. It plays a vital role in stimulating the shark's defense mechanism, which prevents or

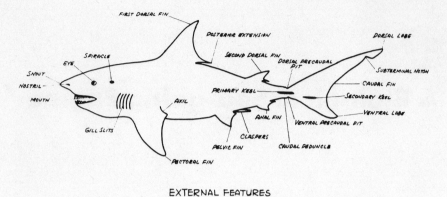

EXTERNAL FEATURES

DRAWING BY CAPT. HAL SCHERR

Illustration of a shark's external anatomy.

delays the invasion of disease. Medical researchers have recently discovered a method of developing a stimulating agent in the form of a serum extract made from the lipid. This extract, when injected into laboratory animals such as mice and chickens, reduces or delays tumor growth to a significant degree.

It was the shark's liver that provided scientists with a better understanding of the defense systems of man. Then other land and sea animals were studied, marking the beginning of further research that eventually led to the development of new serums derived from this common source. The future of man's well-being appears brighter as researchers isolate and purify new substances to combat diseases such as cancer, leukemia, and malaria.

The function of a shark's liver is similar to that of other animals. Its primary purpose is to regulate body chemistry and to control the metabolism of protein intake in the body, which influences the growth process. The liver manufactures bile used in the intestines for digestive purposes and, at the same time, emulsifies fats before they enter the gall bladder for storage.

The liver is the shark's largest organ. Its size, compared to total body weight, far exceeds the livers of other animals. It is constructed of two separate elongated lobes and often comprises one-seventh of the shark's total weight. For example, a 780-pound tiger shark was reported to have a liver weighing 160 pounds. In another case, a 7,302-pound white shark, caught in Cuban waters during the forties, had a liver weighing more than 1,000 pounds.

The size and weight of a shark's liver varies and depends upon the quantity and quality of food available. If one shark consumes nutritious food, its liver will become larger than another whose food is poor in quality. Therefore, a shark that consumes a great quantity of less nutritious food does not necessarily produce a larger liver.

Shari Buxton, student marine biologist, examines the left lobe of the liver of an eight-foot female lemon shark. The large cluster of eggs would have descended into the uterine cavity where further development of each embryo takes place.

Sharks are not really the gluttonous creatures that some people think they are and they sometimes reject food regardless of what is available. Their large livers function like vast storehouses, keeping fat until it is needed. This has been demonstrated by the great number of sharks

WEATHER FORECAST
(SHARK OIL)

As a barometer, shark liver oil played an unusual role in the history of mete-orological equipment. Years ago, before the invention of intricate weather instruments, the people of Bermuda forecast the weather by observing the changes in the character of the shark liver oil standing in a glass bottle. The solubility of the oil alters and it becomes cloudy just before a drop in temperature occurs.

that live for many weeks in captivity without food. In this respect, sharks could be compared with bears and other creatures that hibernate for long periods without eating. A shark stores oil fat in its liver just as a bear stores fat in its liver and tissues to nourish it during hibernation.

In some sharks the liver is enormous and contributes greatly to the shark's buoyancy. A 200-pound shark might weigh only a few pounds if weighed in water. But this is enough to cause it to sink to the bottom. Since sharks do not possess air bladders, most of them are compelled to swim continuously to keep from sinking. However, a few species such as the nurses and lemons can remain almost motionless on the bottom for short periods, depending upon the amount of oxygen in the water.

The shark liver is best known as a rich source of vitamin A. During the forties a multimillion dollar industry emerged in the United States after scientists discovered that shark livers produced a vitamin A of far greater potency than that derived from cod or halibut. The discovery was made soon after the outbreak of World War II when the foreign supply was cut off. American commercial fishermen plunged headlong into this new enterprise that netted them profits they had never enjoyed before. In some instances, depending upon the potency of the liver and the sharp decline of the shark population due to overfishing, prices skyrocketed to as much as $18 a pound. One Florida catch was reported to yield 350,000 units of vitamin A per gram, compared to an average yield of approximately 50,000 units per gram.

But the industry was short-lived and the boom was over by 1947. Research laboratories devised a method of synthesizing a more potent vitamin A that was far less expensive and more palatable than the natural liver oils. People no longer had to hold their noses while supplementing their diets!

I often admire the function and capability of a shark's stomach. This admiration probably stems from the mixed emotions I have about my own stomach. There are many kinds of foods I would like to eat, but I know I would pay dearly for the gastronomical pleasure. If we were endowed with stomachs similar in function to that of sharks perhaps we would be free from many disorders of the gastrointestinal tract. We might not be annoyed with ulcers or have to restrict ourselves to special diets.

A shark's stomach is made up of two connecting parts and each part has a separate, individual function. The first part is called the cardiac stomach; the second is known as the pyloric stomach. The cardiac portion has a unique function; it serves as a combination catch basin and separator. It holds its contents for approval or rejection before releasing them into the pyloric for digestion. Some sort of intricate mechanism (about which little is known) triggers the digestive process and allows the material to pass into the pyloric region of the stomach. Literature cites a number of cases where dissections revealed that the contents of the cardiac stomach were in a good state of preservation and showed little signs of deterioration even after a period of eight days. One noted authority substantiated the finding of a human arm that had been in the cardiac stomach for several weeks but showed only minor signs of decomposition.

Evidently nature intended the shark to scoop up anything that comes along even if it is not usable. The cardiac stomach sorts out the unwanted or indigestable material before permitting it to enter the pyloric stomach. But the amazing part of this "catch-all" is its ability to rid itself of the unwanted contents either by regurgitation or dislodgement of the organ itself. The cardiac stomach is very elastic and the entire organ can stretch and slip out of the shark's mouth, empty its contents without injury to itself from the shark's teeth, and then return to its place in the abdominal cavity. One might compare the process to turning a sock inside out and washing it.

A shark will poke its nose anywhere for a meal. The owner of this primitive lobster trap caught more than he expected. The lobster-hungry lemon met its death when it became trapped in the small opening of the oil drum. (Photo by Paul Brundza)

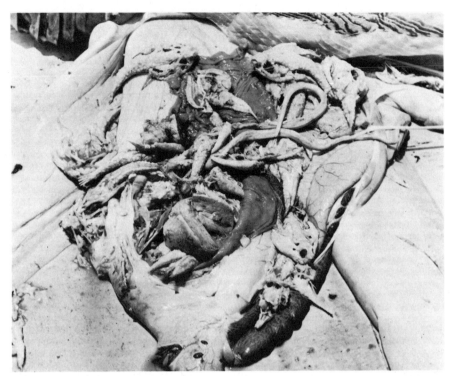

Tiger sharks prey upon large fishes, but they also scavenge the ocean bottom. The stomach contents of this large tiger disclose a gruesome assortment of bottom creatures such as batfish, blowfish, eels, stingrays, toadfish, and the body of a large horse conch with its operculum still intact. The mysterious absence of the conch shell supports the premise that sharks are able to regurgitate unwanted material.

The material that is not expelled evidently passes the "test" and is admitted into the pyloric stomach. It is here that the real digestion begins. This part of the stomach is much smaller in diameter, less elastic, and accepts only edible food. After digestion has taken place, the material passes into the intestines. Dissections of the pyloric seldom disclose any bulky material but only a semiliquid substance known as "chyme" from the process "chymification." This chyme provides the shark's system with nourishment after it enters the intestinal tract.

What do sharks eat? Well, you name it and they will eat it, or at least try. This includes chomping on the trans-Atlantic telegraph cables! Sharks have been known to choke to death while trying to swallow large living or inanimate objects and there is one gruesome case on record where a shark choked to death while attempting to swallow a human being!

Man has about 25 feet of intestines compared to a few feet for the shark. But, I don't think that sharks are afflicted with the colonic disorders of humans such as tumors, diverticulitis, or constipation.

In both mammals and sharks the initial function of the intestine is basically alike. Its primary purpose is to provide nourishment through osmosis and to eliminate waste matter by defecation. In the shark, however, the relatively few feet of intestines operate in an extraordinary way.

If we take a good look at this unique bit of biological engineering we can see that nature has designed an efficient, compact intestine called a spiral valve. There are several versions of this organ in different species of sharks and rays, but most are basically similar in their functions. Although the intestine is short, the apparatus consists of a spiral corridor roughly resembling a coil spring, which provides a greater length in a smaller space. The food particles have a longer way to travel as they move in a circular direction through this alimentary spiral. This enables them to take advantage of the increased absorbent surface which, in turn, increases the efficiency of digestion and osmosis (the process of transmitting nourishment into the bloodstream through a semipermeable membrane, the membrane in this case being the inner intestinal wall). In some spiral intestines the food matter makes as many as 40 turns before reaching its exit. The end result is a spiraled feces that is considered a remarkable curio by collectors but only in fossilized form!

The other extremity of this "biological engine" is known as the "business end" and it is here that the real action takes place. The mouth contains a formidable armory of dentition which makes the shark one of the most respected and feared creatures in the sea. When Mr. Shark flashes his toothy smile it's time to watch out!

The open mouth reveals several rows of teeth—each chiseled to a point. The edges are almost razor sharp, and are serrated in some species (similar to the cutting edge of steak knives), which makes their bite even more effective.

Most species of sharks possess five to seven efficiently arranged rows of developed teeth. However, when looking into a shark's mouth, only the first two or three rows are visible. The remaining teeth are lying flat and partially concealed by a tough but flexible membrane. Since the skeletal structure of sharks is cartilaginous, the teeth are not anchored in their jaws as securely as those of the bony vertebrates. Consequently, many teeth are broken off or lost during natural usage such as biting or tearing at coarse or unyielding material. According to one authority, the floor of the ocean is literally "carpeted with shark's teeth"!

In addition to possessing highly efficient dental equipment, a shark's

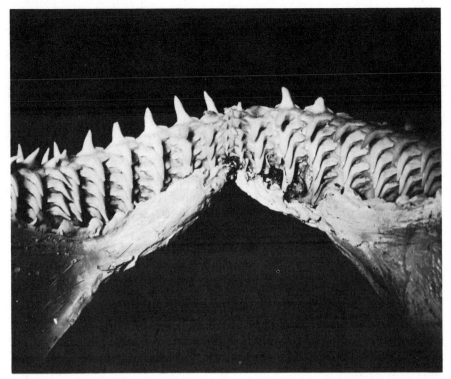

Shark teeth are always cavity free because of the miraculous tooth-replacement process. The membrane was removed from the jaws of this lemon shark to expose the extra rows of teeth.

jaws are powerful, more powerful than most people suspect. Scientists have long known that sharks have extraordinary force in their jaws because many of the attacks upon swimmers resulted in the severance of leg and thigh bones. Human bone is much harder than the wooden planks that sharks have been known to bite in two with little apparent effort. In spite of the fact that a shark's jaws consist of cartilage that is considerably softer than animal bone, the shark is blessed with some mighty strong muscles linked to this jaw structure. When a shark bites, the exerted force is almost unbelievable.

After their curiosity was aroused by the awesome power of the shark's bite, scientists constructed instruments able to measure the force with reasonable accuracy. The results indicate that sharks seven to ten feet long are capable of exerting pressures of as much as three metric tons per square centimeter. This is the equivalent of more than 6,000 pounds on an area less than one-half inch square! Truly incredible power!

In spite of a mouthful of shark teeth and powerful jaws, it is hard to believe that a shark can execute a bite so easily. This impression comes from observing the position of the mouth. It is located well back and under a long snout. Because of this, a theory was advanced years ago that a shark had to roll onto its side in order to clamp its jaws on anything. After enough people had witnessed sharks feeding, this theory was abandoned.

What actually occurs when a shark makes a grab for an object can best be described as follows: its underslung jaw, which is nearly concealed, juts out forcibly from its head; the hideous jaws and teeth come into full view when the mouth opens, while the snout is elevated and drawn back until it becomes nearly vertical to the body. With its teeth bared, the shark is now in a position to make a head-on bite. This gruesome countenance causes the most hardened sharker to shudder and is the main cause of the shark's unpopularity throughout the world.

However, it is not looks alone that make it unpopular. Frequently, I have seen (always from a comfortable distance) a shark grab at its prey. Most of these observations were made while one of my customers was fighting a fairly good-sized game fish. Usually, the shark would zoom suddenly from the depths and take a chunk out of the fish struggling at the end of the line. With one bite, the shark could sever what might have been a potential trophy fish. It is a frightening moment when the rending, crunching sound of many teeth ripping into living flesh becomes audible. It is even more awesome when the battle takes place on the surface where it can be seen as well as heard. However, it is the actual physical movement of the shark's jaws, from their hidden position, that strikes me as an incredible feat.

Nature was generous and wise in providing the shark with several sets of formidable cavity-free teeth. I'm sure it's no accident that there is a close resemblance between shark's teeth and the minute toothlike projections called "dermal denticles" that are firmly anchored in its hide. These denticles receive nourishment in the same way that the teeth in the shark's mouth do—through a pulp canal that contains nerves and blood vessels. Anatomically speaking, these denticles are considered scales (placoid). They do not take part in any sort of replacement process and are a permanent part of the shark's skin.

The resemblance between the denticles on the hide and the teeth in the shark's mouth ends, however, when we begin to discuss the replacement factor. The shark not only has inherited a set of noncarious teeth but, in addition, it also has a multitude of extra ones. It has been my personal experience in examining countless numbers of shark teeth that there is no decay.

Unlike most land and sea animals, baby sharks are born with a complete set of workable choppers so they can begin to forage for food immediately after birth. Like the teeth of mature sharks, the teeth of the juveniles also function as both defensive and offensive equipment.

A hungry lemon shark grabs an offering head-on, dispelling the old belief that a shark must turn on its back to bite an object. (Courtesy Wometco Miami Seaquarium)

Although the enamel-like covering is just as hard and impervious to damage as the teeth of bony fish or other members of the vertebrate kingdom, there is a slight difference in its chemical composition. This might account for some of the absence of decay or other kinds of deterioration in the tooth structure. On the other hand, since the tooth replacement process is so efficient the teeth may not have had time to develop any noticeable defects.

The nurse shark is no Florence Nightingale. Its small teeth and strong jaws are especially adapted for crushing purposes. The two appendages hanging below the eyes (called barbels) function as tactile organs. The creature's thick, tough skin (almost impervious to injury) is valued highly by the commercial shark-fishing industry.

The actual length of time the replacement process takes has recently been discovered in an unusual experiment. One authority claims that tooth replacement occurs periodically regardless of loss or damage in the act of feeding or while in conflict with its enemies. We do know that a shark seems able to produce thousands of teeth during a normal lifetime. Scientists recently made a detailed study of the growth and rate of tooth replacement in young captive lemon sharks. One group was given an unlimited food supply. Another group was starved. While they were temporarily anesthetized, their upper and lower jaw teeth were measured and tooth movements plotted on charts. It was concluded that the well-fed lemons replaced their upper jaw teeth at the fantastic rate of one tooth every 7.8 days per dental unit! The lower jaw teeth were replaced a little less frequently. In the starved lemons, the tooth replacement rate in both upper and lower jaw averaged approximately 10 percent longer.

In conclusion, we find from these experiments another example of nature's mysterious preservative talents at work and an interesting area for dental researchers to explore.

Although almost all fish accomplish reproduction without bodily contact between male and female, sharks reproduce in much the same way as mammals. Fertilization is achieved only through sexual intercourse.

Aristotle was one of the first to describe the reproductive process of the sharks inhabiting the Mediterranean Sea. The reproductive mechanism of sharks intrigued scholars of Aristotle's time after the unusual similarity to amphibians and mammals was recognized. It was also discovered that the sexual behavior of sharks was more advanced and organized than the fish and that it closely resembled the sex life of the mammals. In all species of sharks, copulation was achieved by intercourse, the insertion of the male's clasper (a penislike appendage) into the female's cloaca (an orifice similar to the vagina in mammals).

The natural sex act among sharks is usually confined to the open sea, but there have been rare instances when copulation took place in captivity. On these occasions, the acts were recorded on film and scientists suspect that a pair of copulating sharks might even achieve an orgasm when the male's seminal fluid is injected into the female's oviduct.

To insure the perpetuation of these species, nature had no inhibitions about endowing the male shark with adequate genitalia. Unlike any other member of the animal kingdom, the male shark possesses *two* functional claspers. The reason for the double equipment is not fully understood; there are two schools of thought as to their implementation. Some scientists speculate that, in some species, both claspers are thrust into the female since she has two vaginal-like orifices. Another theory, based on eye-witness reports, suggests that only one clasper is used at a time. Lemon sharks have been observed to remain *in copula* for almost an hour using only one clasper. In other species, copulation lasted from 15 to 30 minutes. So far, it has not been established how long a male must wait before he is able to perform an encore—or a double encore!

Another similarity between sharks and mammals is the secretion of a lubricant (a generous amount, since water can easily wash away the substance) prior to the insertion of the male clasper into the female. The canals in the claspers are connected to two muscular bladders (whose function was only discovered recently) called siphon sacs. Each sac produces and expels the necessary mucous secretion to facilitate an easy entry into the female.

The male's sex cells (spermatozoa) are contained in the testes located between the stomach and spinal column and are conveyed via a long tube called the *ductus deferens*, which connects to the groove

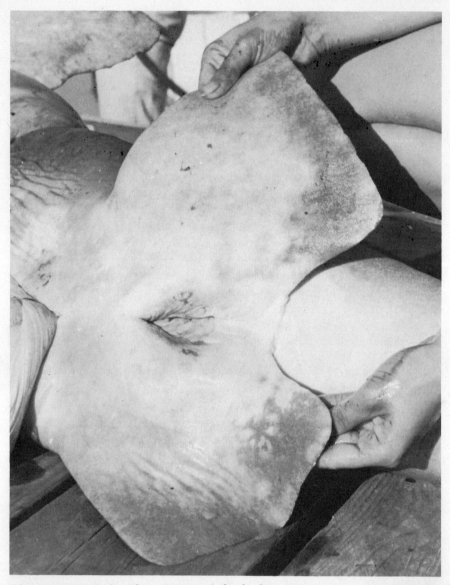

The female genital orifice of a nurse shark also serves as an excretory outlet.

on the inner side of each clasper. The spermatic fluid is assisted in its travel by the motion of hairlike flexible projections called cilia found in the lining of the *ductus deferens*.

Since copulation takes place while sharks are swimming, the males of many species have a rigid hooklike claw on each clasper which serves as a holding device and keeps the female oviduct open while insemination takes place.

Years ago, Dr. Daniel Merriman of the Bingham Oceanographic Laboratory at Yale University gave what is probably one of the clearest explanations of reproduction in sharks:

There are three different types of embryonic development in sharks, depending upon the species:

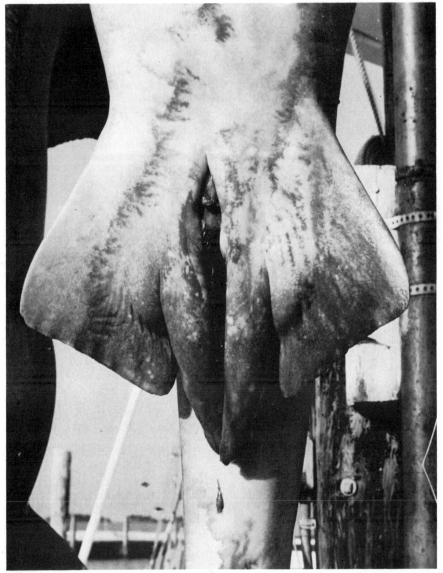

The male reproductive organs of a nurse shark. Every male shark has a pair of these penislike appendages called claspers.

The twin siphon sacs of the male shark are located in the abdominal cavity slightly forward of the cloacal aperture. Each sac contains the necessary mucous secretion to assist the flow of seminal fluid through the claspers, facilitating the impregnation of the female.

(1) In one type, the shark lays eggs that hatch outside the body. A shell is formed around the developing egg and the egg is laid at an early stage in the growth of the embryo. Hatching occurs considerably later and in much the manner in which a chick hatches from its egg, but of course under water. Sharks that produce their young in this fashion are called *oviparous*—in other words, they are brought forth from an egg.

(2) Some sharks give birth to living young. Here the developing embryo has an attachment to the wall of the uterus, a connection comparable to, although not exactly like, the placental arrangement in humans. Sharks that reproduce in this fashion are said to be *viviparous* ('born alive').

(3) The remainder are hatched from an egg while it is still in the body and undergo further development in the oviduct before being born as miniature adults. The embryonic shark in this case is nourished by a yolk sac attached to it and also from the nutritive fluid in which it is immersed. The embryo never has a placental attachment to the mother, and they lay free in the oviduct or uterus. After the yolk is absorbed, it is possible that they nourished themselves by swallowing the unfertilized eggs that lay close to them in the genital tract. Sharks that produce their young in this fashion are called *ovoviviparous*, that is, they hatch from an egg but undergo further development inside the mother before being born alive.

Several years ago biologist and shark authority Stewart Springer was the victim of a rare phenomenon that authenticated the only known case of intrauterine cannibalism in the animal world. Sand tiger sharks are ovoviviparous and claim the weird distinction of being cannibals before they are born. The eggs are hatched in the uterus and the young remain there until they are fully developed before leaving the mother. Since there are two separate uteri, only two young pups will be born. A matter of "first hatched, first served" takes place as the newly hatched young immediately start devouring their weaker brothers and sisters for their sustenance as they emerge from other eggs. While Springer was examining the uterus of a pregnant sand tiger, his hand was bitten by an unborn pup!

The gestation period of sharks varies greatly and depends upon the species. Some are born after an eight-month development while most require 14 months before they can emerge into the water. The dogfish has the longest gestation period among the vertebrates, taking 20 to 24 months to develop.

Bill Hanna and Floyd Stinson display some well-formed hammerhead pups. A Caesarean section delivered 25 pups, each measuring 24 inches in length. Their 750-pound mother was 14 feet long. (Photo from Florida's Game Fish and How To Land Them, *South Brunswick and New York: A. S. Barnes and Co., Inc., 1968)*

The size of the litter also depends on the species involved. The great hammerheads are able to have as many as 30 pups, while tigers have been known to bear over a hundred. Lemons, sandbars, duskys, and bulls have three to 15 young at a time depending upon the age of the female. Sand tigers, again, will bear only two pups at a time. The females of most species bear a litter only once in two or three years.

People are always fascinated with the biological structure of sharks, especially the man-eating variety. Stomach dissections disclose all sorts of strange creatures although I have never found any human remains. I have found everything from beer cans to conch shells and, on one occasion, the remains of a small dog. People are also intrigued by a shark whose reproductive organs resemble those of the mammals and, in some instances, of man.

There are so many fascinating features in a shark; their organs function so much more efficiently than other creatures that many

A lemon shark bearing a pup. Most species of sharks deliver their young alive and the pups are left to fend for themselves, if they can evade mother's hungry jaws. When pups are born, they are completely developed and able to fill their role as predators. (Courtesy Marineland of Florida)

A one-hour-old baby tiger shark born in captivity that measured 24 inches. (Courtesy J. W. LaTourrette, Wometco Miami Seaquarium)

people are beginning to appreciate this fine mechanism that took nature 300 million years to perfect.

Dr. Perry W. Gilbert, one of the nation's leading authorities on sharks and their behavior, has conducted extensive studies dealing with the visual acuity of sharks. Results of his studies show that sharks are able to see better than most scientists thought. He found that the retina contains many light-sensitive rods that assist in the visual sensitivity of the eye.

Although the eyes of most sharks are comparatively small, they are able to distinguish objects at considerable distances if a strong contrast exists in the background. They can see in dim or brightly lighted conditions, but in many cases are unable to discern the color of an object or most of its details.

When the intensity of light is low, sharks are able to see exceptionally well. This is due to the special construction of the eye. The area in back of the eye acts as a mirror and reflects light back through the retina, adding additional stimulation to the eye's light-sensitive rods. As in the eyes of a cat, the pupils are vertical and slit shaped in strong light and become circular when they dilate in the dark to allow more light to enter. The eyes of a shark respond quickly to changes in light and can adjust to use in turbid water.

Labeled the "keenest nose in the sea," a shark's olfactory organ (sense of smell) is its chief means of finding food. Its unique ability to detect odors at great distances, places it in a category far above most other marine animals in tracking down a food supply. Almost two-thirds of a shark's brain consists of olfactory lobes and the centers of the smelling senses.

The olfactory pits or nostrils of shark are not used for breathing purposes and are set wide apart under its snout for maximum reception. Since a shark is usually swimming at all times, a constant stream of water is forced over the sensory nerves lining the nostrils. These nerves are connected directly to the brain where discrimination takes place.

In testing the olfactory limits of sharks, scientists discovered that sharks are capable of detecting one part of human blood in 10 to 100 million parts of water. And, incredible as it may seem, further tests have revealed that sharks are able to detect a few drops of blood in water almost a 1,000 yards away and can follow the scent to its source!

Another sensory organ that permits a shark to locate its prey is called the lateral line or lateris system. Also found in the fishes, this sensorial mechanism is able to detect movement or vibrations in the water at considerable distances. The system consists of a line of minute tubules that lead from surface pores to canals under the skin, running the length of the body from the tail to the head and around the snout. The pores contain small tubes called neuromasts, which house sensitive filaments or clusters of sensory cell-like hairs. The canals contain a fluid that moves when a sound wave strikes it. The movement of the fluid, in turn, causes the hairs of the neuromasts to move or to become stimulated (depending upon the intensity of the disturbing sound wave) and creates a nerve impulse that leads to the brain, automatically registering the pressure of the activity or moving object. Low frequency vibrations created by thrashing fish attract a shark and permit it to "home in" on the source of the commotion.

Another feature of this unique organ is its ability to detect the presence of a fixed object or a motionless fish in the water. The position is *felt* from the shark's own movement through the water, which creates a vibration that reflects off the object and returns to the emitting source—the shark's lateris system. This unusual function is. called "distant touch" by scientists and can be compared to electronic underwater detection gear such as sonar.

Coupled with the lateris system of sound-and-motion detection, a shark's ears provide further assistance in its relentless search for food. The ears consist of two small channels (the saculus and lagena) lined with sensitive hairs imbedded in a jelly like material. The organs are located inside the head and are able to detect high frequency sounds while the lateris system confines its function to a lower frequency range. So the shark's two separate and distinct hearing mechanisms provide it with the uncanny ability to locate any kind of movement or activity in the water.

Since low frequency sounds travel farther in water, nature provided all its marine creatures with hearing mechanisms that detect only the lower range of sound frequency. The hearing of sharks ranges from 1,000 down to only 7.5 cycles per second and become extremely sensitive at 40 to 60 cycles per second. In contrast, the range of human hearing measures from 16,000 to about 40 to 100 cycles per second.

The blood of sharks plays an important role in laboratories where studies in cancer research are being conducted. Scientists have discovered that the primitive (but double) system of immunity found in shark blood is more potent against infection than the more advanced immunity known to exist in the blood of man. This means that sharks possess both specific and nonspecific antibodies that defend their systems against any foreign substance or virus, while man's defense mechanism is limited and, in many cases, incapable of destroying the viral invader.

When cancer cells are mixed with shark blood serum, the cells are destroyed. Bacteria and viruses are also killed. This peculiar immunity enjoyed by sharks is one of the major targets of immunological studies conducted by medical researchers.

The shark (the most primitive animal known to produce antibodies), ironically, produces only one of the three classes of antibodies produced by man but the shark manufactures about 10 times as much, making its defense equipment far more efficient than man's.

The incredible survival of the shark probably hinged directly upon this type of antibody. The other two classes that were added to the more complex physiological makeup of man were not required.

New findings about antibodies in shark blood serum are currently under study. The substance "infantile proteins" that provides human infants with disease immunity, soon breaks down and disappears with age while sharks retain the immunizing agents throughout their lives.

Scientists are on the threshold of finding out why sharks, which are virtually unchanged by 300 million years of evolution, are so advanced in their ability to reject the invasion of cancer and even the common viruses that have plagued man and animal for centuries.

Respiration in sharks is essentially the same as that of the fishes except for the difference in structure. Both require water to pass over their gills so that oxygen can be absorbed into their bloodstream. However, depending upon the species, a shark may have five to seven sets of gills while a fish has only one. Accordingly, pound for pound, sharks probably require more oxygen to maintain their metabolic balance than fish. In addition to their gills, sharks possess an auxillary respiratory organ called the spiracle, which is located directly behind each eye. This is a small aperture that allows water to flow in, and is believed to assist in providing oxygen for the brain and the eyes.

The skeletal structure of sharks is totally cartilaginous but the lack of hard bone does not necessarily create a burden or deprive the creature of any of its functional abilities. After 300 million years of adjustment and adaptation to an environment that changed continually, the shark is probably superbly equipped to meet any severe change in the future. Physiologically, the shark might be better suited to its habitat than the bony fishes.

Although the cartilaginous material is a primitive characteristic in sharks, it contains hard gristle (manufactured by certain proteins) greatly reinforced by fibers. It is more elastic than bone and therefore more compressible and resistant to shock and breakage. Apatite, a mineral substance composed of carbonates and calcium phosphates, is strategically located in areas of the skeleton where any points of stress may come into play, such as the vertebrae associated with swimming movements.

The age and the life span of sharks are two more of the many mysteries surrounding this creature. Few sharks have been able to survive captivity for any great length of time, which makes age determination most difficult. So far, no biological features have been found that can offer a definite clue to a shark's age. Modern literature cites few longevity examples; studies in this area are being conducted continuously.

Because of their well-built structure and efficient organs, sharks probably live longer than we suspect. Very few sharks have been found dead from natural causes or diseases, and all seem to thrive successfully except when their environment is changed by captivity. Scientists have captured large female sharks that possessed senile characteristics and found that their ovaries had stopped functioning, but no age could be established in these particular studies.

The growth rate of sharks varies and depends greatly upon their environment, size, and the availability of food. Among the larger species of sharks such as the great whites, growth studies revealed that they can reach eight feet in length within two years. Tigers, too, seem to grow quite rapidly and will reach seven feet within two years. Lemons have been found to reach six feet during a three-year period. According to a tagging study, dogfish reach maturity after 10 years, measure approximately 24 inches, and have a probable life span of 25 to 30 years.

Almost every book or report that has been written about shark behavior has mentioned the remarkable insensitivity to pain demonstrated by these seemingly indestructible creatures. Official records are bulging with accounts by people who have caught sharks and found them extremely difficult to destroy. Sharks have been bludgeoned, shot, perforated, drowned, eviscerated, and damned only to revive and swim nonchalantly away to their mysterious haunts.

Many of these tales, which have the flavor of sensationalism, are in fact often true and are substantiated by documentary evidence or backed by affidavit certification.

An excellent example comes from Morris Vorenberg, president of the famous Palm Beach Sharkers, an enthusiastic group of shark anglers who fish for sport. Vorenberg, a dedicated shark expert with 20 years of experience in this field is a valued consultant for the Smithsonian Institute. In his unpublished book, *What About Sharks?*, he writes of a true personal experience bordering on the incredible:

"Only recently I completely eviscerated a ten-foot nurse shark which had been caught on rod and reel, removed its liver, stomach, and intestines and then tossed it overboard. The shark fell on its back into the water, sputtered a few times, then turned over into a swimming position and placidly made its way into deeper water. About fifteen minutes later another fisherman had a hard hit on his baited hook. When the fish was reeled in it proved to be the previously gutted nurse shark."

Vorenberg possesses an affidavit signed by three people who witnessed the occurence, confirming the accuracy of the incident.

There are many other records that prove a shark's unusual resistance to pain and death—cases that all testify to its strong will to live outside of captivity.

Another good example that illustrates a shark's unusual immunity to pain took place several years ago aboard my charter boat. I was shark-fishing in the offshore waters of the Florida Keys when one of my customers hooked a large sand shark. After a 20-minute tussle, my angler skillfully maneuvered it alongside for me to dispatch. Since there was no tournament in progress whose rules would disqualify the catch if firearms were used, I fired my .38 caliber pistol at the brain of the shark. The slug hit the shark's head but, apparently, missed its small brain. Before I could get off another shot, it turned tail and sounded swiftly, running off 100 yards of line and leaving a blood-stained trail in its wake. The angler worked the shark over again but, before he could get it half way to the boat, the hook pulled loose and the shark was free. From the glimpse of the creature we guessed that it might have weighed about 200 pounds.

We baited the hook with another live yellowtail snapper and resumed fishing. About a half hour later, the same angler had another strike and set the hook. After a short time, he had the shark alongside and we discovered, with astonishment, that it was the same shark!

Blood was still oozing from the bullet hole in the side of its head. This time I fired two shots, one of which smashed its brain completely. We were amazed at this rugged predator whose insatiable appetite proved greater than its sensitivity to pain!

Some sharks are able to attain unbelievable speeds. Although none are thought to be as fast as some of the bony fishes like the tuna, dolphin, or the billfish, several stomach dissections revealed that these swift gamesters were caught and devoured by makos, whites and porbeagles. These sharks, however, are the swiftest of the entire clan and have been accurately clocked up to 40 miles per hour. Since tuna and dolphin have been clocked at 60 miles, one can guess that only the sickly ones that lagged behind their school were caught and became easy prey for the fast-moving sharks.

Most sharks are slow-moving creatures and only the few that have just been described as swift species possess the strong caudal peduncle (the narrow body section located forward of the tail) and lunate tail (consisting of a keel on each side) that provides stability. Their bodies are compact and streamlined making them almost hydrodynamically perfect.

Locomotion in all sharks is similar since their forward movements depend wholly upon the propulsion created by their tails. The tail fin also enables the shark to turn to the left or right. Unlike the bony fishes, the shark's rigid pectoral fins do not assist it in motion but provide stability and serve as a planing device similar to the gear used by submarines. The pectorals function only to provide a quick change in pitch to point the shark's body up or down. The dorsal and anal fins prevent the shark from rolling and yawing.

Over the years, scientists have found that a definite and complex social organization exists among sharks. For example, large, medium, and small sharks of each species will form individual groups and travel their separate ways; otherwise, the larger will predate upon the others, and the medium-sized will prey upon the small. Normally, sharks of equal size seldom exhibit any aggressive action toward each other unless one is wounded and then a feeding frenzy may occur. As a result of these social orders, specific nursery areas have been singled out by gravid females that bear their young and then leave to return to their own groups to feed.

The range and distribution of sharks is a vast and complex subject and, for unknown reasons, some species exhibit such erratic migratory patterns that contradictions are often encountered in a study of a particular species.

Tagging programs, instituted and supervised by scientists have removed portions of the mysterious veil hanging over the movements and habits of some sharks species. Thousands of anglers, too, cooperated with the scientists in expanding their studies dealing with shark migrations. Anglers were provided with tagging kits and instructions and later were informed of the results of a particular tagging program.

One of the most active scientists studying the growth, population and migratory habits of sharks is Dr. John G. Casey of the Department of the Interior, Bureau of Sport Fisheries and Wildlife. Dr. Casey has done a remarkable job in popularizing shark-fishing as a sport and has enlisted the enthusiastic cooperation of anglers whose tagging efforts contributed valuable data to his studies.

One tagging program involving 8,000 sharks resulted in 222 recoveries (more are expected) and included 33 species. Among the pelagic species, blue sharks were found to be extensive travelers. One particular blue migrated over 1,700 miles to Venezuela, South America, where it was recaptured. It had taken 64 days to make the journey, which meant it had averaged 27 miles per day! Another interesting recapture in 1970 off Venezuela was a mako tagged off New England in 1967. A black-tipped shark was recaptured after making an 800-mile journey between Florida and Vera Cruz, Mexico. Sandbar sharks too, are long-range migrants. One champion tagged off New Jersey in 1965 was recovered six months later off Flagler Beach, Florida. As a rule, sandbars are usually limited to a 150-mile range.

Anglers interested in shark-fishing who wish to cooperate in these tagging programs can contact Dr. Casey at the Narragansett Marine Game Fish Laboratory, Narragansett, Rhode Island.

Tagging sharks can provide the angler with an unusual hobby and the excitement of the possibility that his tagged shark may be recaptured later, hundreds of miles away. In addition, he will be assisting scientists in important research studies that will eventually be advantageous to mankind.

A shark is a strange creature indeed. The fact that it has been roaming freely for more than 300 million years may account for its difficult adjustment to captivity. At times its behavior completely baffles the scientists who are searching constantly for reasons. For the scientist trying to conduct his research, it is important that a shark react as naturally as possible in its captive environment. Marine attractions, too, have problems keeping sharks alive in captivity and must keep their sharks on exhibit as long as possible to reduce the frequency of expensive collection trips. After sharks are captured (by rod and reel or by the commercial longline and nets) their inanimation is apparent.

Most sharks, after they have been removed from their natural habitat and plunged into a man-made environment, usually die regardless of how slight their injuries may be. Death seems to come swiftly to those sharks that lose their spirit or lack the will to live. Immediately after capture, some sharks will settle down to the bottom of the holding tank and appear to be sulking. Actually they are in the silent

Dr. John Casey, fishery biologist, carefully attaches an identification tag to a shark's dorsal fin. (Courtesy Dr. John Casey)

throes of slow suffocation. Almost all species exhibit a similar reaction to captivity, but some resist *any* life-sustaining assistance. Other species make the best of the situation. These include some of the lemons, nurses, duskys, and an occasional tiger (among the larger species).

All sharks lack a swim bladder; therefore, it is necessary for them to be in continual motion in order to receive the life-sustaining oxygen from the water that flows through their gills. Newly captured sharks usually have to be "walked" by attendants to force the water through their gills, a procedure akin to artificial respiration. This means that one or two courageous attendants will hold onto the shark and literally pull it along through the shallow water in the tank.

Many captured sharks often refuse food and must be fed by force—either by stuffing food into their gullets or by intravenous infusions. As a safety measure, an anesthetic is sometimes administered before they are force-fed. However, as indicated by the high mortality rate, all these methods often fail.

Because a shark has always been cast as the proverbial "diabolical villain," possessing extremely agressive tendencies, literature often reports: "sharks have no mortal enemies except man and porpoise." But, in reality, sharks have many more enemies, even themselves. Cannibalistic by nature, many sharks are so fond of their own flesh that mother sharks will gobble up their own offspring as soon as they leave the safety of their bellies!

Killer whales are known to include sharks in their diet of seals, fish, penguins, etc. Stomach dissection of these rapacious beasts furnish conclusive evidence that sharks sometimes are a chief source of food when the whales pause in their travels to feed.

Squid, too, are the shark's enemies, especially those giant species lurking in the deep waters of the Humboldt Current off the coast of Peru. Their thick tentacles are studded with powerful suction discs that can grip and hold a shark to prevent it from swimming. This cuts off the oxygen supply it normally receives from the water floating through its gills. The squid then feeds upon its victim by ripping it to pieces with its strong parrotlike beak. Sharks, marlin, swordfish, and small whales are known to be victims of this scarce and ferocious monster that seldom makes an appearance except at night. Even 50-foot whales, which were fortunate enough to escape the deadly embrace, were found covered with scars made by the suction discs of a giant squid.

The larger billfishes such as the swordfish and the marlin are also mortal enemies of the shark. A few sportfishing captains and big-game anglers have seen these huge creatures fighting each other far out at sea. Billfishes are notorious for their speed and maneuverability and can ram their hard, pointed bills into a shark's vitals. While attacking, they are able to dislodge their bills by backing off, gathering speed and repeating the onslaught any number of times until their victim is rendered helpless.

But, next to man, the porpoise appears to be a shark's chief enemy and, in turn, the shark becomes a hostile opponent of the porpoise. In most cases the shark is the aggressor—by provocation—and winds up

Sharks are cannibalistic even in captivity. This lemon shark was sickly and had difficulty adjusting to its new environment. It was attacked and thoroughly eviscerated by its hungry companions. (Courtesy Wometco Miami Seaquarium)

on the defensive.

For years, extensive research has been conducted on the shark-porpoise relationship. The program has been accelerated recently and attempts are now being made to train porpoises to act as bodyguards

Captain Charles Buie, collector for the Miami Seaquarium, captured this 300-pound bull shark. Buie demonstrates the evidence of a rare attack by a sailfish upon a shark. From the size of the bill protruding from the shark, the sailfish (a much smaller adversary) must have weighed only 50 pounds. The shark survived without lasting ill effects; its wounds were healed completely at the time of its capture. It was alive and on exhibition for several days before its death from unknown causes. (Courtesy J. W. LaTourrette, Wometco Miami Seaquarium)

to divers in shark-inhabited water. Although results of these studies are still inconclusive, it is still generally known that sharks and porpoises will tangle for various reasons. Many seafarers have reported seeing these conflicts in the open sea; some were probably exaggerated. However, enough sightings were made by reliable eye-witnesses to substantiate the reasons for the bloody feuds that often result in death to either opponent.

A school of hungry sharks sometimes attacks one or more porpoises, especially if they are small or have become separated from their main community. Sharks will also threaten a female porpoise while she is in the throes of labor or giving birth to her young. Usually the female is well protected if she has many companions and they are organized enough to discourage the threat of an attack. Or, it could be the other way around, with more and larger sharks than a small group of porpoises can handle.

On occasion, sharks and porpoises have been seen swimming peacefully side by side. They have also been found feeding upon the same school of frantic mackerel.

Usually, sharks and porpoises living together for long periods in the same tank at a public aquarium ignore each other completely. Since they are well fed and adjusted to captivity, apparently their natural instincts are suppressed and therefore they exhibit little animosity.

As a rule, porpoises seldom behave aggressively. They lead a carefree and pleasant existence and practice a "laissez-faire" policy. But, if a shark interferes with their normal living habits the porpoises attack the predator—charging and butting their hard snouts into its gills and soft underbelly—a shark's most vulnerable zone.

I had always considered these shark-porpoise vendettas legendary until I personally witnessed a rare and brutal attack upon a shark about 10 years ago.

We were trolling the offshore reefs of the Florida Keys when we came upon a heavy concentration of king mackerel averaging about 10 pounds. We were catching them one after another, when suddenly a school of 20 to 30 small bottle-nose porpoises appeared and began to chase the kings. As my customer was reeling in a king, one of the porpoises zeroed in on the struggling fish and swallowed it.

There was no holding this powerful rascal. He ran off most of the line and began jumping and spinning in midair. We could see that he was well hooked and in pain since he was bleeding from his mouth and wailing mournfully. Unfortunately, there wasn't much that we could do but cut the line and hope for the best. Just then, we spotted a 12-foot hammerhead shark cruising boldly toward the injured porpoise. Either the hammerhead had picked up its distress cries or its blood scent. The predator got no closer than 50 feet when the entire school of porpoises gave up their chase for the kings and surrounded its helpless companion with a wall of protection. The shark veered from its course, turned tail and retreated. Several of the porpoises broke rank and charged after the hammerhead, launching what appeared to be a well-organized attack.

Amazingly, these sagacious little creatures took turns, swimming off and, then, gathering up speed, swiftly ramming the hammerhead with their hard noses. We could hear the thumping sounds made by the forceful impact of bone against flesh. The huge shark shuddered and squirmed in agony under this merciless onslaught. Several times it tried to jump out of the water but only foundered and convulsed at the surface as the bombardment by the angry porpoises continued. Thick streams of blood gushed from its mouth, clouding the surrounding water. In a few minutes the violent carnage was over. The crushed hammerhead began its death spiral—sinking slowly—and finally disappeared in the crystalline depths leaving a twisted crimson trail behind.

I don't know what happened to the hooked porpoise. As soon as its companions finished off the shark, they all vanished from sight. The porpoises were small in comparison to the hammerhead but, because of their intelligence and community-minded traits, they achieved unified strength. The hammerhead weighed at least 600 pounds, while those agile and powerful little creatures couldn't have weighed more than 150 pounds. It was certainly a strange and bizarre conflict and we, who had a "front-seat" view of this macabre performance, were stunned by this manifestation of nature's grimmest law!

I am not entirely sure of the shark's true function in the sea but I do believe that nature must have placed it there to serve some useful purpose related to maintaining the balance of living things. Man, with his clumsy strategy, often upsets nature's balance and later pays dearly for it.

Knowledgeable people, who claim to be well grounded in ecology and marine science, appall me with their endorsement of shark extermination. Like all-knowing pedagogues they sit in judgment, insinuating that the ocean and its creatures would be better off without these "repulsive" animals. Fortunately, however, the majority of scientists view such an irrational suggestion with alarm and assert that sharks have a definite, important place in the sea. It is ironic that two such separate and divided schools of thought exist among these intelligent people.

Aside from my special interest in the critters, I agree with those who believe that sharks have an important role in our oceanic society.

Some scientists believe that sharks make a worthwhile contribution to the hygiene of our marine environment by reducing natural pollution. In addition to pursuing live fish, most sharks are fundamentally natural scavengers. Nature endowed them with rugged digestive organs

Gerald Scott, Nova Scotian fisherman, exhibits his 12-foot white shark. Scott discovered the huge shark helplessly entangled in his salmon net. Because the occurrence of this man-eater in the almost totally landlocked area of the Minas Basin is so rare, the catch made newspaper headlines and scientific journals. (Photo by Hattie Densmore)

that tolerate substances most marine creatures reject. Consequently the shark reverses its position and becomes a benefactor to our ecology and a part of nature's balance in the sea.

An excellent example of this turnabout usually takes place after a "red tide" has killed a great number of fish. In one instance, sharks by the hundreds were discovered gorging themselves upon acres of floating, decaying fish. Although miles of beaches were still covered with dead fish, sharks *did* have a part in reducing the number that was carried in by the wind and current.

The red tide is a natural but rare phenomenon that occurs only in the warm seas of the world. A sudden population explosion takes place when free-drifting organisms congregate in large masses because of certain changes in weather and water conditions. The mortality of marine life is high. Countless rust-colored organisms steal the life-giving oxygen from the water and give off a toxin; both factors are responsible for the mass extermination of fish. Biologists speculate that sharks may possess some immunity to the toxin. Because a lack of oxygen could be detrimental to them, sharks probably feed upon the fish only after the expiration or dissemination of the organism.

4

Sharks Are *Not* Worthless

A LIVE, HEALTHY SHARK THAT CAN BE EXHIBITED IS PROBABLY FAR MORE valuable than the sum of its salable parts. Special techniques must be used to capture a large shark without inflicting serious injury, and a knowledge of the shark's physiological makeup is necessary to keep it alive in captivity for a reasonable length of time. The task of capturing some of the open-ocean or pelagic species could be far greater than trapping a rare and wild jungle animal for exhibition at a zoo. Because of people's growing interest and obsession for sharks, millions of dollars are spent by marine attractions to display these formidable creatures to the public.

Live sharks have become a fascinating feature not only in aquariums but also in night clubs. One of Europe's largest (the new Holiday Inn) in Munich, Germany, has a three-story night spot built into a gigantic salt water tank. Sharks and night-clubbers eye each other through the portholes as the guests enter the "Yellow Submarine" by way of an underwater tunnel. The club's tank includes hammerhead, lemon, and sand sharks—captured and flown to Munich via jet cargo plane from the Atlantic Ocean and the Gulf of Mexico.

When a shark is dead, its skin can be valuable, and it is in constant demand by the leather goods industry. After sharkskin is treated (by a complicated process known only to a few tanneries throughout the world), the leather becomes a soft, attractive, and durable material used in the manufacture of expensive shoes, belts, briefcases, boots, and other products that are usually made from the skins of other animals.

According to the U.S. Government Bureau of Standards, sharkskin is the strongest leather known—it has a tensile strength up to 7,000 pounds per square inch. Cowhide, next, will test at approximately 5,000 pounds per square inch.

Because of the successful development of synthetic vitamin A that

Dave Powell, curator of fishes at Sea World, and assistant haul a blue shark up the chute into the transport box. The shark will be kept alive by a respiratory mouthpiece during its speedy trip to the marine attraction. (Photo by Nancy Chase, Sea World)

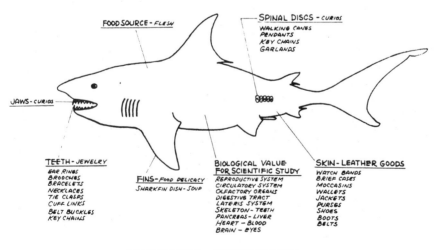

FOOD SOURCE - FLESH

SPINAL DISCS - CURIOS
WALKING CANES
PENDANTS
KEY CHAINS
GARLANDS

JAWS - CURIOS

TEETH - JEWELRY
EAR RINGS
BROOCHES
BRACELETS
NECKLACES
TIE CLASPS
CUFF LINKS
BELT BUCKLES
KEY CHAINS

FINS - FOOD DELICACY
SHARKFIN DISH - SOUP

BIOLOGICAL VALUE
FOR SCIENTIFIC STUDY
REPRODUCTIVE SYSTEM
CIRCULATORY SYSTEM
OLFACTORY ORGANS
DIGESTIVE TRACT
LATERIS SYSTEM
SKELETON - TEETH
PANCREAS - LIVER
HEART - BLOOD
BRAIN - EYES

SKIN - LEATHER GOODS
WATCH BANDS
BRIEF CASES
MOCCASINS
WALLETS
JACKETS
PURSES
SHOES
BOOTS
BELTS

COMMERCIAL COMPONENTS

DRAWING BY CAPT. HAL SCHARP

Commercial shark-fishing can be profitable when most of a shark's components are utilized.

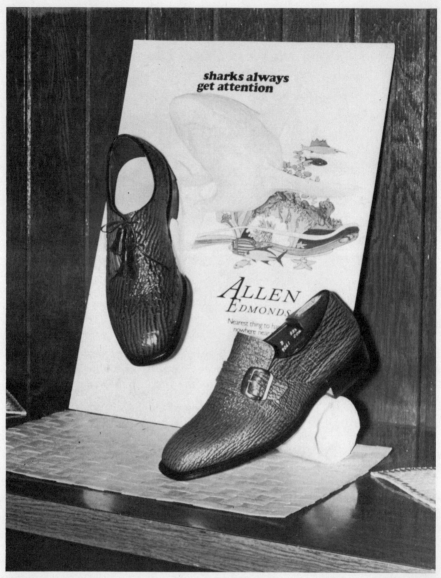

Attractive and durable sharkskin shoes have the distinctive appearance of exclusive footwear.

began 20 years ago, commercial shark-fishing was almost completely abandoned. Since shark livers were no longer in demand, what little fishing that still flourished was solely for the purpose of obtaining skins for leather products. Now that the shark is recognized as a valuable food source (in addition to its biological value for scientific study, marine attractions, and a source of material for the manufacture of specialty jewelry), the U.S. government is encouraging the resumption of the shark-fishing industry in U.S. waters. An informative booklet called *Shark Fishing Gear: A Historic Review* (circular 238) that describes the equipment and techniques employed in catching sharks,

Early photo of a centrifuge in operation during the commercial shark-fishing boom. The machine separated the sediment from the heavy shark liver oil before the final processing for commercial distribution.

can be obtained free by writing to the Office of Information, Bureau of Commercial Fisheries, U.S. Department of the Interior, Washington, D.C. 20240.

Commercial shark-fishing can be profitable when almost all of a shark's body can be sold. Like any other business, plans and details worked out on paper always seem to promise easy profits, until the plans are put into actual practice. To make shark-fishing pay, full or part time, the would-be operator must first explore the market demand. This means contacting tanneries as prospective buyers for hides, biological supply houses for the organs, gift shops and the jewelry trade for teeth, and finding an outlet for the flesh.

The few commercial shark fishermen who operate successfully in this country market their flesh in a number of ways. Some who are equipped for quick-freeze and processing methods, have contracts with foreign countries that purchase shark meat for human consumption. Others have made a profit selling their meat to fertilizer plants or to the local crab fishermen who find shark meat ideal as bait for their traps. Another possible use for shark meat is the conversion into protein fish meal. This outlet,however, requires detailed investigations and consultations with government agencies dealing with food products and processing.

Some biological supply firms like to keep a good stock of shark teeth

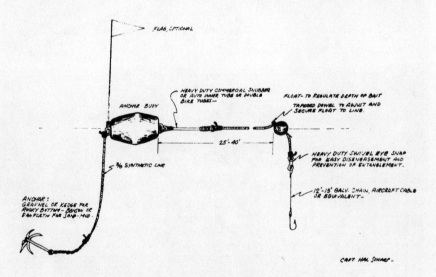

SHARK FISHING GEAR (DRAWING NOT TO SCALE)

This single hook shark-fishing method, when used in quantity and distributed over a large area, will catch more sharks than a longline containing an equal number of hooks.

Governor Claude Kirk inspects an exhibit prepared by the Florida Marine Research Laboratory, illustrating the value of shark skins. The governor would like to see the revival of the commercial shark-fishing industry in his state. (Courtesy Florida Board of Conservation)

on hand. These are usually used for classroom study and should be cleaned meticulously before they are sold.

Gift and souvenir shops, too, want shark's teeth for the tourist trade. Some shops make their own trinkets and jewelry but an enter-

prising shark fisherman might devise an original item that will catch
the eye of the public and manufacture his own line to sell to the shops.

Shark's teeth are easy to remove from the jaw. Simply boil the jaw
in a mixture of lye (caustic soda) and water. A small amount of lye
will do a good job, but it depends upon the size and number of jaws
and the quantity of water in the container. With a little experimenting, an effective formula can be found. Extreme care must be exercised
to prevent personal injury; proper gloves should be used since lye is
a deadly poison.

Complete shark jaws are also in demand by biological firms and
gift shops. Nicely cleaned jaws will sell for $5.00 for a six-inch jaw
and up to $50.00 for a 24-inch jaw. Properly identified jaws mounted
on an attractive wall plaque will naturally bring a better price.

Shark teeth are studied for several reasons other than determining
which species has attacked an unfortunate victim. Fossilized teeth are

*Necklaces and earrings made with tiger shark teeth are popular gift shop
items. (Courtesy Tropic House Gifts, Marathon, Florida)*

Captain Hansen and his assistant, specimen collectors for Seaquarium, engaged in removing the hook from a thrashing tiger shark caught by longline methods. The vessel's huge live well serves as an ideal holding tank until the sharks arrive at their new home. (Courtesy Wometco Miami Seaquarium)

important to the palentologist's study of primitive sharks. Many collectors of shells and other marine specimens consider teeth an important addition to a fascinating hobby. Some hobbyists concentrating on fossilized teeth devote much of their time to combing coastal beaches and excavating inland pits for rare or unusual specimens to add to their collections.

Shark's teeth have been used in many strange and ingenious ways. Pacific Island natives fashioned crude weapons (spears, daggers, and swords) studded with shark teeth that they used in battle with enemy tribes. Even today, on some islands, similar weapons are made but they are used only for ceremonial purposes such as commemorating special or ancient rites. Since the cutting edges of the teeth in some species are extremely sharp, these were employed in the development of ancient surgical instruments. Trinkets of shark's teeth were worn or used for bartering purposes. For centuries, shark's teeth have been used in these ways, contributing to the culture of the island societies.

Recently shark's teeth have become a popular commodity in the trinket and jewelry industry. Nearly every first-class coastal gift shop has an unusual and attractive assortment of jewelry on display. Earrings, bracelets, rings, pins, cuff links and tie clasps are inexpensive, useful souvenirs. Some teeth, plated with gold or silver, are in a class of special distinction.

Another source of income for the commercial fisherman can be derived from shark's blood. Some biological companies need a permanent source to obtain blood smears which are used by schools for study and analysis and in medical research laboratories. Prices vary slightly among the companies but the pay seems adequate and, as a sideline, I found it to be profitable. Supply houses can be contacted by obtaining their addresses in McRae's Blue Book directory or the Thomas Register found in any public library.

With care, a small three-foot shark can provide enough blood for 1,000 smears. The shark must be alive when the blood is extracted so that the cells are mobile when coagulation takes place. To reduce the movements of a writhing shark, pacify it by spraying its throat or gills with MS 222 Sandoz (Tricaine Methanesulphonate), an anesthetic that can be purchased in aerosol form or a 0.1% solution mixed in sea water. After the shark is calm, make a small puncture in the caudal vein located on the ventral side of the tail. The blood can be drawn by either a hypodermic syringe or an eye dropper depending upon the efficiency of the operation.

Unless they specify otherwise, biological supply houses usually request the white blood cell differential count laboratory procedure in preparing a shark blood smear. Using the eye dropper or syringe, place one drop on the slide. Spread the blood thinly and evenly with the edge of a second slide (held at an angle of 30 degrees or less to the surface of the first). Slides must be thoroughly dry before packing for shipment and extreme care should be taken to prevent dust or other foreign particles from settling upon the slides. Depending upon their particular requirements, the supply houses will advise if a stain should be used.

In addition to investigating the olfactory organs and the circulatory system, scientists conduct extensive research on other organs of the shark such as the heart, liver, brain, and pancreas. Some of these studies pertain to the development of an effective repellant or a deterrent to insure the safety of air and sea disaster survivors; other tests deal with medical research. Both are important to the welfare of mankind.

Sometimes the biological supply houses that furnish research laboratories with shark organs will need a number of them in stock. In order to utilize the shark as much as possible, a commercial shark fisherman should inform the supply companies of the availability of shark organs. In this way he can supplement his income with little added effort.

Even embryos are occasionally in demand for study in school classrooms. In addition, embryos (preserved in glass jars filled with alcohol or formaldehyde) are popular in some gift shops and retail for as much as $5.00 each.

A commercial shark fisherman often catches pregnant female sharks that can provide him with an extra bonus if he takes the time to remove the embryos and place them in attractive jars. Most female species will carry five to 12 young but the tiger can average as many as 30 to 50 beautifully marked embryos. Large hammerheads, too, are notorious for bearing big litters containing 20 to 30 young and, because of the odd shape of their heads, are fascinating subjects for display.

Although shark is popular table fare in countries where food supply is short, it also delights the palates of people in countries renowned for their sophisticated cuisines. Unfortunately, the majority of Americans have never cultivated a taste for shark—knowingly.

Along the West Coast shark fillets are consumed in great quantities under the names of "grayfish" or "whitefish." Eastern seaboard restaurants often feature swordfish steaks when, in reality, their clientele are smacking their lips over the mako shark, the texture and flavor of which closely resemble the highly prized sword. "Sea scallops," too, are sometimes devoured by Americans who don't realize that they are eating shark or ray whose savory flesh has been "punched" out in the shape of the sea scallop.

Yes, it *is* ironic that Americans cannot accept shark under its true label. They show no aversion to consuming many kinds of domestic and wild land animals or almost any other type of marine creature. Their prejudice *must* stem from a loathing for man-eaters, even though the shark's reputation has been grossly exaggerated. Yet Americans will eat all sorts of creatures found on the shelves of supermarkets and gourmet shops. Canned hippopotamus, camel, and elephant (each animal kills and injures more people yearly than sharks) sell for $4.00 to $6.00 per pound and are rapidly gaining in popularity. Insects, too,

Shark embryos are not only used for classroom study; they also have recently become popular specimens for sale in many coastal gift shops.

have titillated the palates of many people who find chocolate ants, caterpillars, and baby bees delightful tidbits. (Records reveal that more people are killed in this country by bee stings than by sharks!)

Nearly 1,800 people are bitten by rattlesnakes every year in the United States. Almost 100 of these prove fatal. Still, you are not with the "in" crowd of epicures unless you relish the meat of these reptiles.

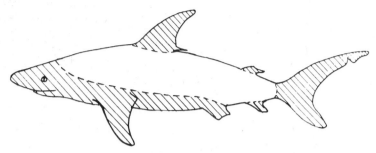

The unshaded area of the drawing depicts that portion of the shark recommended for food utiliztion.

In some areas canned rattlesnake sells like hot cakes! Seafood (such as snail, eel, octopus, and squid) long featured on foreign menus is growing in popularity with Americans who are learning to enjoy the flavor of these repulsive-looking creatures.

Every year Americans consume thousands of tons of cold cuts (some-

A package of dried gelatin made from processed shark fins. This material is the principal ingredient in the famous Chinese shark-fin cake, shark-fin soup, and shark-fin dish.

times called "head cheese") made from ground-up pig snouts, tongues, cheeks, hoofs, and ears stuffed in the animal's casing! The brains of cattle (sweetbreads) and their stomachs (tripe) are all popular food supplements to the American diet. Even "chittlins" (strips of pig's intestines fried to a crisp) activate American salivary glands.

Food experts agree that shark meat, when properly processed, is a tasty, highly nutritious food. Shark can be cured, fried, broiled, baked, or chowdered. The appearance and texture is actually more appealing than some fish, and, with a little imagination in its preparation, its flavor can be greatly enhanced.

Why do Americans avoid shark meat? Simply because education and publicity are lacking. If a demand existed, the commercial fishing industry would be delighted to include shark in their catches. But before the industry will invest great sums of money to gear their methods to catching sharks on a large scale, they require assurance that a demand for the meat exists. The special, expensive procedures required to process shark meat make it economically unfeasible now. Evidently the industry does not feel that it should invest in a costly campaign to "sell" the public on eating shark as long as an abundance of other seafoods exists.

A commercial shark-fishing business may very well head that long list of oddball businesses considered least likely to succeed. At one time during the early forties, before vitamin A was synthesized, shark-fishing was a booming industry. Oil from shark livers is rich in vitamin A and the precious liquid was then far more valuable than imported Scotch whiskey. In those days anyone who could handle a boat or raft and had a back strong enough to strike hard when the critter grabbed a baited hook, could make an easy dollar. It still takes a strong back, but now, real business knowhow is also necessary to convert merchandise such as shark flesh, skins, fins, and teeth into groceries on the table.

Commercial shark-fishing isn't exactly big business but it is not a kid's game either, as discouragement and disappointment are always encountered. Fighting rough seas and inclement weather, maintaining a boat and expensive equipment, risking a hernia or the loss of a hand (the brutes are heavy and love to bite!), or fighting the objection made by indignant community leaders who are repulsed by the idea of this kind of business operating in their community, could easily force a man to throw in the towel and be content with sweeping floors for a living.

So what does it take to go into the shark-fishing business? A special kind of person—a stubborn, persistant individual, one who has good business sense and enjoys the tough challenge that only this type of occupation offers—a man who doesn't shrink from long hours and back-breaking work and is still able to keep his pencil sharpened. Tough requirements? Yes. That's why there are very few of this breed around.

Although spiny dogfish are popular as a food source in many foreign countries, they are considered a nuisance by commercial fishermen along the northeast coast of the United States and Canada. At one time, attempts were even made to exterminate this wholesome fish which has the potential of good table fare. (Courtesy Robert K. Brigham, National Marine Fisheries Service)

Les Rayen (Capt. U.S. Army, retired) formerly a tough and seasoned paratrooper now captains his own fishing vessel. How he made the jump from the corps to shark-fishing for a living came about almost by accident.

Basking sharks awaiting slaughter and the rendering of their oil. (Courtesy Irish Tourist Board)

Since much of his service was spent in the tropics, when retirement time came he decided to forsake the cold climate of Massachusetts and move his family south to enjoy the warm weather of Florida. Having puttered around boats all his life, he set his sights on something much lower than air duty, such as sea-level work. Rayen thought it would

be great to operate a sportfishing charter boat and make a living pulling big-game fish from the blue waters of the Gulf Stream.

He roamed the waterfronts of Florida's east coast looking for that
special spot in which to begin a fishing operation. One day in Ft.
Pierce, Rayen met two Cuban refugees, experts in shark-fishing who
had plyed their trade successfully in their homeland during pre-Castro
times. Shark hides brought a fair price at the tannery if one did not
mind the grueling hours of setting and recovering long lines in
weather that would make the salty skipper of a 10,000-ton freighter
cussing mad.

After taking a few sharky excursions with his new friends, Rayen
became intrigued with the monsters. He decided to pitch in and learn
the fascinating business of removing one of man's oldest and most
mysterious enemies from the ocean and convert them into greenbacks.

In a few months he felt that he had enough experience to strike
out on his own. He purchased a surplus navy launch and converted
it into a real productive "shark-snatching machine, a major job that
took ingenuity and a lot of sweat. Soon his longlines were hooking

At the bow of the Tiburon, *Captain Rayen prepares to harpoon a large shark
swimming near the surface.*

sharks at the rate of 6,000 head per year. This meant that the manufacturers of leather products could supply the growing demands of fashion-conscious customers. A leather tannery which claims that it alone knows how to process shark hides was pleased with Ryen's production record and gave him the exclusive franchise for the sale of shark hides in Florida.

The news of Rayen's shark-catching talents spread up and down Florida's east coast. One community, whose citizens were alarmed by a sudden outbreak of shark attacks upon swimmers, realized that the tourist dollar could be in jeopardy and tried to persuade Rayen to move his operation to its area to reduce the shark menace. This town, believing that it had an excessive shark population in their waters, did not feel obligated to offer Rayen any worthwhile guarantee to justify his expenditures if he made the move. He declined the overture and continued work on his long-range plans for establishing a large commercial shark-fishing industry at Ft. Pierce.

One of Rayen's most recently completed projects is the retail store located on U.S. Highway 1, a few miles north of Ft. Pierce, called

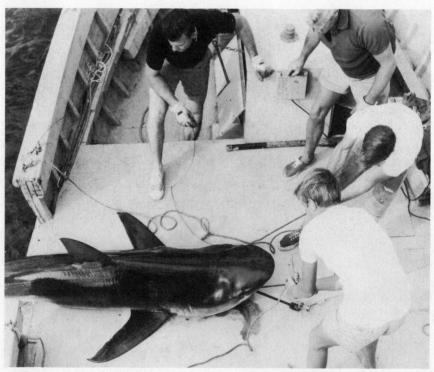

All hands pitch in to haul a large yellow shark on deck. This species is considered rare, and positive identification has not been established.

Captain Rayen skillfully removes the skin from a freshly caught shark. Leg burns and abrasions caused by brushing against a shark's rough hide occasionally become infected.

Capt. Les Rayen's Shark World. This unique shop is possibly the only one of its kind in the world. It carries a complete and exclusive line of shark leather products such as shoes, wallets, belts and purses, and a fine selection of unusual shark jewelry. It also features a vast collection of fossil shark teeth for the hobbyist. One entire wall of the store

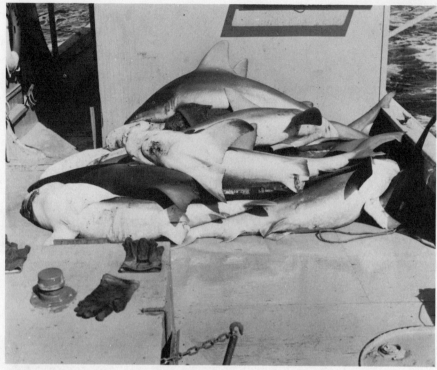

A typical day's catch aboard a commercial shark-fishing vessel. The sea has yielded some of its most treacherous creatures in the interests of medical research, food products, leather goods, and jobs for men who are not afraid of hard work.

is covered with a breathtaking display of man-eating shark jaws for those who desire to purchase a trophy or conversation piece for their dens. Other household articles with a nautical flair such as lamps, bookends, shells, and table decorations are also featured in this unusual store. Even a whole mounted man-eating shark of any size caught on one of Rayen's longlines can be ordered from this extraordinary store and shipped anywhere in the world.

Rayen is currently working on plans for building a large plant to process shark flesh, which is highly nutritious and a popular food in some countries. He will also construct a laboratory and library for visiting scientists who wish to conduct on-the-spot experiments. The U.S. government and the United Nations are aware of Rayen's work and have requested that he provide facilities for rotating personnel each month to learn his fishing and processing techniques. These observers will return to their own countries to develop commercial shark-fishing, which will in turn alleviate severe food shortages.

A documentary film is now being considered that will give Rayen's

Carl proudly displays a properly "beamed" skin, which is now ready for the curing process.

projects worldwide publicity. The local county and industrial development commissions are cooperating with him toward the establishment of a research center for federal agency personnel to assist in many future shark studies.

5

Danger Stalks the Depths

DURING PEACETIME, THOUSANDS OF PEOPLE AROUND THE WORLD ARE killed or injured every day by many causes. Newspapers are filled with the accounts of victims who are involved in auto collisions (a number-one killer), ship sinkings, air crashes, train wrecks, hold-ups, poisonings, and countless injuries (many are fatal) that take place in their own homes. People are killed or maimed by explosions, tornados, fires, earthquakes, lightning, venemous and nonvenemous insects and reptiles, and by wild and domesticated animals. The list of causes is endless.

Sharks too, are responsible for the mutilation and death of human beings. However, in comparison to the great number of other tragic events, shark attacks play only a minor role in the appalling list of grim statistics. As man-killers, sharks even rank far below bees, scorpions, and mosquitoes. A rough tally of the causes that kill or disable people throughout the world during a given day would reveal that shark attacks account for much less than one out of every 1,000 casualties.

Why does a shark attack—an occurrence that takes place with less frequency than almost any other kind of incident that may injure or kill a person—make newspaper headlines? The answer may be in the deceptive nature of the incident or the horrible manner in which a live human being is torn and mutilated by a wild, blood-thirsty creature that inhabits the domain on the edge of an unexplored and mysterious frontier.

For centuries the word *shark* has gripped and terrified people, causing them to shudder at the creature's formidable reputation as a consistant man-eater. Even today, with our increased knowledge (scanty as it may seem) of the creature and additional safety measures to repel it, the word still holds an ominous and frightening spell over us. So, perhaps this is the reason why a shark attack always hits the front

Newspapers headline the menaces of sharks along with their uses in scientific research.

page. After all, there are not many wild creatures on land that will deliberately pursue man to satisfy their appetites.

Regardless of how insignificant shark-attack statistics may seem compared to the great number of other injuries, a human life is involved and its preservation is still all-important to society.

The documented shark-attack file that was originally compiled by the Division of Fishes, Smithsonian Institution, Washington, D.C., is a veritable storehouse of information pertaining to shark attacks throughout the world. Since its inception in 1958 piloted by Senior Zoologist Dr. Leonard P. Schultz, a research team processed information received by several worldwide newspaper clipping services. Then the researchers were able to follow up the reports, verify their accuracy by investigating the incidents, and incorporate the results in a permanent file.

In 1969, the project was terminated at the Smithsonian Institute and the file (now called The International Shark Attack File) was transferred to the Mote Marine Laboratory, Sarasota, Florida. Dr. Perry W. Gilbert, one of the world's foremost authorities on sharks and attacks is the director of the laboratory and is also chairman of the

Dr. Perry W. Gilbert, executive director of the Mote Marine Laboratory, Sarasota, Florida, and chairman of the Shark Research Panel of the American Institute of Biological Sciences, which coordinates shark studies in all parts of the world. One of the world's foremost shark authorities, Dr. Gilbert is renowned for his prolific literary output and for his studies of shark attacks and shark behavior.

Shark Research Panel of the American Institute of Biological Sciences.

There are many cases of shark attacks that never reach the news media. In some instances, the news of the incidents are suppressed because of the unfavorable publicity that might result for those engaged in businesses that depend upon coastal tourism. As a result, knowledge of these attacks sometimes never reaches the investigators. In these cases, they would appreciate the cooperation of persons who were involved in any way with the incidents.

Shark-attack investigators also solicit volunteers to assist them in the field, either persons associated with statistical data concerning shark attacks or those who reside in an area of potential attacks.

The accumulation and documentation of all this information is a realistic approach to learning more about the mysterious ways of sharks. Based upon this vast collection of statistics and the circumstances surrounding the attacks, many questions concerning the reasons why sharks attack people may be answered in the near future. In addition, the data becomes part of many important shark-attack studies made by the members of the American Institute of Biological Sciences Shark Research Panel. The results of these studies assist science and technology in providing practical and up-to-date safeguards for swimmers and divers against attack. Completely effective repellents and survival equipment will someday become realities.

A questionnaire is used by researchers in collaboration with shark-attack investigators in the field. It was designed for efficient tabulation and covers most of the essential facts pertinent to a shark attack. The form is circulated widely throughout the world to persons connected in any way with attacks. All information is studied and later documented, becoming a permanent part of the original official shark-attack file.

Anyone who is involved in or has any knowledge pertaining to a shark attack can report the incident to the International Shark Attack File, c/o Captain H. D. Baldridge, U.S. Navy, Mote Marine Laboratory, Sarasota, Florida, or contact Mr. M. Vorenberg, 2111 N. Flagler Drive, West Palm Beach, Florida, Telephone 833-8739.

Mr. Vorenberg is a field investigator and consultant for the Shark Research Panel, American Institute of Biological Sciences, and will be happy to assist in the preparation of the questionnaire.

Medical consultants examine what could be part of a human pelvis. The fragment was found in the stomach of a shark by Captain Hansen, specimen collector of the Miami Seaquarium. (Courtesy J. W. LaTourrette, Wometco Miami Seaquarium)

Since shark attacks occur under various conditions and unusual circumstances, the worldwide attacks listed in the International Shark Attack File are divided into five categories:

(1) UNPROVOKED ATTACKS: All cases in which sharks have, without provocation from man, made deliberate physical contact with the victim or with the gear he was wearing.

(2) PROVOKED ATTACKS: All cases in which sharks were caught, trapped, speared, injured, or provoked by man in some other way, and in which they attacked as a result of this provocation.

(3) BOAT ATTACKS: All cases in which sharks, whether provoked by man or not, deliberately made physical contact with a boat, life raft, water ski, or equipment being used in the operation of a boat (oar, propeller, etc.).

(4) AIR AND SEA DISASTERS: All cases in which sharks, unprovoked by man, have eaten or mutilated victims of such disasters who were or may have been alive when attacked.

(5) DOUBTFUL ATTACKS: All cases in which sharks, unprovoked by man, have approached swimmers but have failed to make physical contact with them; all cases reported as "attacks" with subsequent investigations tended to discredit or place in doubt; all cases in which the victum is known to have been dead before he was attacked.

Each of these categories clearly indicates the manner of the attack and serves as a starting point for researchers to analyze and develop a statistical conclusion. These facts obtained from the shark-attack questionnaire aid researchers to search for the reasons that stimulated the shark to attack. A summary of all the facts is tabulated and recorded. Knowledge gleaned for this information could eventually result in the development of effective repellents and deterrents.

A study of case histories of shark attacks upon people can reveal some mighty gruesome and discerning facts. For example, during the five-year period from 1962 to 1967, sharks attacked 637 people without provocation. Of this number, 161 attacks were made upon swimmers, divers, and surfers along inshore waters. Over 40 percent (70) of these attacks were fatal. The offshore toll was greater. In the wake of sinking ships and air crashes, sharks attacked 476 people with 350 fatalities resulting. Since there is no way of determining the number of people who were still alive when these attacks occurred, the figure is somewhat speculative but considered official.

During this same period, the records show that sharks attacked 30 small boats, but there were no fatalities involved. Sharks also attacked

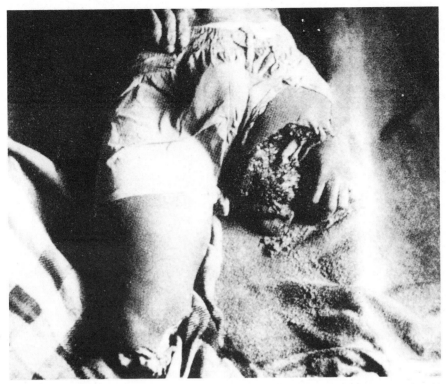

This fatal attack upon a male victim, age 22, took place on a South African beach. Both legs were amputated. From the shark-tooth fragments found in the wounds, the species was identified as a Zambezi shark weighing about 400 pounds and approximately nine feet in length. (Courtesy Oceanographic Research Institute, Durban, South Africa; Journal of the Royal Naval Medical Service)

26 divers and swimmers who deliberately provoked the sharks but none of these incidents was fatal.

In analyzing the geographical locations of shark attacks during this five-year period, the records indicate that 32 of the 161 unprovoked attacks that occurred in inshore waters took place along the coast of the United States; Australia had 22 and The Republic of South Africa has 16. The rest of the attacks occurred along the coasts of Mexico, New Zealand, Taiwan, Japan, Hawaii, Bahamas, Bermuda, Phillippines and Fiji Islands, India, Italy, and Greece.

According to the official records, a shark can attack at any time of the day or night and in practically any kind of water condition, although the majority of these attacks took place in water temperatures

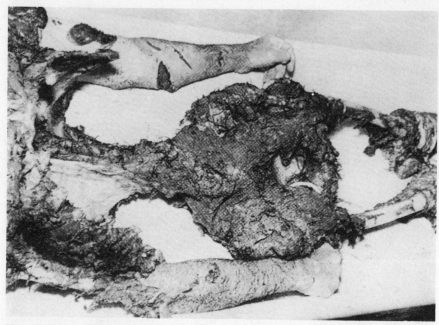

Here is an anterior view of extensive damage by sharks upon the body of a drowned victim. The 40-year-old male was recovered on the following day with most of the flesh removed except for parts of the lower legs, forearms, and head. The nature of the teeth marks on the arms suggests a cutting type similar to those of the Zambezi shark. (Courtesy Oceanographic Research Institute, Durban, South Africa; Journal of the Royal Naval Medical Service)

about 68°F. Therefore, most attacks occurred in the temperate and tropical zones of the world.

There is little doubt that a great number of attacks throughout the world are not on record. Coastal countries that lack efficient communications and news media are unaware of or have little knowledge of the exact number of attacks upon their people. Every year, scores of natives are attacked and killed by sharks off wilderness coasts far from civilization. So, in reality, the number of officially recorded shark attacks is not really large when we consider the great number of attacks that take place unknown to the authorities.

Further inquiry into the vast stockpile of records will offer some idea of the number of attacks made upon people during an average year. Consultants speculate that (including the unrecorded and vague number of attacks made upon the primitive peoples of the world) as many as 300 persons are either killed or injured each year without apparent provocation. This figure does not include the number of attacks made during wartime or any major marine disaster, which can increase that number considerably.

Captain William Gray, director of collections at the Miami Seaquarium, applies a temporary bandage to deep gashes caused by a bull shark attack. The attack occurred while Captain Gray was assisting in the transfer of the bull from the channel to a holding tank. Fifty-seven stitches were required to close the wounds. (Courtesy Wometco Miami Seaquarium)

The old maxim "dead sharks are never dead" still holds true in many cases. I'm not sure that a delayed shark attack can be considered a "provoked" attack especially when the assault was caused by reflexes after the shark was presumed dead. The definition of a "dead" shark could be broad and it would be difficult to say where to draw the line

if there were any question about the nature of the attack and if it were
to be officially recorded as an authentic incident.

Almost any seasoned commercial fisherman can relate one or more
stories of bizarre encounters with "dead" sharks and show a few scars
to illustrate the point. Some have lost their fingers or one of their
limbs because they assumed that the shark was dead.

Many anglers are bitten by "dead" ones while removing hooks from
sharks that have been caught, bludgeoned to insensibility, and left to
rot. A good number of these attacks are reflexes triggered by nervous
spasms that can occur long after death. Any angler, after viewing a
shark's dental equipment, can see the danger of trying to remove his
hooks prematurely.

In most cases when a provoked shark attacks a boat, the damage is
relatively minor. However, when a shark attacks a boat and the boat is
sunk, that's big news!

Al Bayles, jovial owner of the Bayles Boat Yard in Marathon,
Florida, likes to tell about a frightening incident that occurred only

*A hooked enraged shark will often attack a boat even after it is gaffed. This
bull shark charged the boat and bit the propellers, twisting one blade out of
shape.*

This salvaged commercial fishing boat sank after a shark attack. The hooked raging shark charged the boat and tore a plank loose by biting the corner of the stern.

a few years ago. He received an S.O.S. from a boat off one of the out islands of the Florida Keys and sent help to save it.

A man and his wife were fishing commercially when a large shark grabbed one of their baited hooks. Unable to control the angry beast, they stood helplessly as it began a violent attack upon their 35-foot converted shrimp trawler. The boat shuddered as the shark ground its teeth and shook the corner of the boat with such force and violence that it pulled a one-inch plank away from its fastening. Water poured in swiftly through the transom and the trawler began to sink. The frightened fisherman started his engines and ran his boat at top speed until he went aground on a shallow reef nearby.

It was a close call. Their engine compartment flooded and the power shut off just before they reached safety. Fortunately, the boat's momentum carried them up on the reef in time.

During the best part of his 50 years, Bayles has raised, salvaged, and repaired everything from plush cruisers to beat-up derelicts that even a grumpy old grouper wouldn't call home. But he had never before repaired a boat that was sunk by a shark!

Another classic example of a shark attack upon a boat took place about 20 years ago. Two lobstermen were pulling their traps from the rough seas off Cape Breton Island, Canada, when a large shark attacked their small dory. Several planks were stove in and the dory began to sink. One lobsterman drowned and the other clung to the wreckage until he was rescued.

The shark made no further attack upon the lobstermen; perhaps he became discouraged by a mouthful of splintered wood. It was later identified as a great white from the teeth imbedded in the wreckage. It was estimated at about 1,000 pounds and must have measured at least 12 feet in length. The incident made newspaper headlines and Paul Calle, well-known painter, later re-created the tragic drama on canvas.

The centrums or discs, parts of a shark's spinal column, are made of cartilage. The barely discernable rings found in the concave surfaces are expected to offer a clue in determining the age of some species.

Rudy Scharp, holding a scalloped hammerhead shark, shows the grotesque shape of its head. Although there are several species of hammerheads, each can easily be identified by the details of its head structure.

From data compiled by the Shark Research Panel of the American Institute of Biological Sciences, we also find that almost any shark can be dangerous under certain conditions and especially when the critter is provoked. There are, however, quite a few species of sharks that are regarded as more dangerous than others and, usually, will attack man without the slightest provocation.

In many cases, investigators have been able to ascertain the shark's exact identity after an attack. Based upon these findings, and according to the frequency of the attacks, the U.S. Navy researchers went one step further and "rated" the ferocity of some of the leading attackers.

Included in its instructions to their divers and frogmen, the navy's manual (*General Principles of Diving*) lists information on a dozen sharks with ratings from "minimum danger" to "maximum danger." These danger ratings were scientifically and dispassionately evaluated and can be considered absolutely dependable.

Since only a dozen sharks were rated, the reader might assume—erroneously—that only these sharks are dangerous ones. It must be made clear that the navy manual offers only examples based upon some of the leading attacks on file and does not imply that those unlisted sharks are harmless.

From the vast amount of research by shark-attack authorities, a set of safety rules was compiled for people who swim in waters inhabited by sharks. Experts agree that the behavior of sharks is not clear and is still under close scrutiny. In particular, little is known about the obscure reasons that trigger a shark into making an attack. There are so many factors involved—variables related to a shark's environment and its peculiarities that distinguish it from other species of the family—that it has become a controversial subject among experts throughout the world.

These rules cannot absolutely guarantee a person's safety and do not apply to all situations. However, for the time being, until more is learned about the idiosyncrasies of the culprits, the following precautionary measures are recommended when the appearance of a shark is likely or an attack is possible. These rules are endorsed and proved by veterans—people who have sustained encounters with man-eating sharks and/or actual attacks. Let us hope that we can learn from their hard-earned and shocking experiences.

1. Never swim alone. With one or more companions, there is a better chance of summoning help to assist in warding off the attack or of reaching shore and receiving first aid.

2. Do not swim at night. A shark's appetite is greater during the dark hours. A shark appears to be more restless and aggressive while prowling in search of food.

3. Avoid swimming in water with poor visibility. You will be unable to see any sharks if they are in the area and they might be able to spot you first. Although their eyesight is known to be poor, they possess keen sensory equipment that can locate you quickly.

4. Blood attracts sharks like honey attracks bees. Do not enter

U. S. NAVY "SHARK DANGER" RATINGS

Name	Danger*	Maximum Size	Appearance†	Behavior	Where Found
White Shark	4+	30 ft.	Salty brown to black on back	Savage, aggressive	Oceanic; tropical, subtropical, warm temperate belts, especially in Australian waters
Mako Shark	4+	30 ft.	Slender form; deep blue-gray on back	Savage	Oceanic; tropical and warm temperate belts
Porbeagle Shark	2+	12 ft.	Dark bluish gray on back	Sluggish except when pursuing prey	Continental waters of northern Atlantic, allied forms in north Pacific, Australia, and New Zealand
Tiger Shark	2+	30 ft.	Short snout, sharply pointed tail	Can be vigorous and powerful	Tropical and subtropical belts of all oceans, inshore and offshore
Lemon Shark	2+	11 ft.	Yellowish brown on back; broadly rounded snout	Found in saltwater creeks, bays, and sounds	Inshore western Atlantic, northern Brazil to North Carolina. tropical West Africa
Lake Nicaragua Shark	2+	10 ft.	Dark gray on back	Found in shallow water	Fresh water species of Lake Nicaragua
Dusky Shark	1+	14 ft.	Bluish or leaden gray on back	Found in shallow water	Tropical and warm temperate waters on both sides of Atlantic

Name	Danger*	Maximum Size	Appearance†	Behavior	Where Found
White-Tipped Shark	3+	13 ft.	Light gray to slaty blue on back	Indifferent, fearless	Tropical and subtropical Atlantic and Mediterranean. Deep offshore waters
Sand Shark	2+	10 ft.	Bright gray-brown on back	Stays close to bottom	Indo-Pacific Mediterranean, tropical West Africa, South Africa, Gulf of Maine to Florida, Brazil, Argentina
Gray Nurse Shark	3+	10 ft.	Pale gray on back	Swift and savage	Australia
Ganges River Shark	4+	7 ft.	Gray on back	Ferocious, attacks bathers	Indian Ocean to Japan; ascends fresh-water rivers
Hammerhead Shark	4+	15 ft.	Ashy-gray on back; flat, wide head	Powerful swimmer	Warm temperate zone of all oceans incuding Mediterranean Sea, out at sea or close inshore

SOURCE: *General Principles of Diving*: Marine Life–Sharks. U.S. Navy manual.

* 1+ means minimum danger, 4+ means maximum danger.

† All sharks listed are of some shade of white on the under side.

the water with any kind of open wound or partially healed sore that might open up in the water. Women should avoid the water during their menstrual periods. Spear-fishermen should remove their fish from the water immediately and not tow their catches with them while hunting.

5. Do not antagonize, spear, or try to ride a shark regardless of size or apparent disposition. These are wild animals and, as such, will react aggressively in their own defense.

6. Do not panic. (Easier said than done, but this restraint *can* save your life!) After sighting a shark, if you thrash and kick about in an attempt to get away, you could most certainly arouse its curiosity and/or appetite. Try to remain calm and leave the water as quickly as possible, with a minimum of commotion by swimming with steady and rythmic strokes. If diving with scuba gear, remain submerged until you are able to crawl into your boat but always try to keep the shark in view. If the shark makes an aggressive approach, it can sometimes be discouraged or frightened off by releasing air bubbles from your tank.

7. If a shark is in close range and determined to attack, hit it firmly on the snout (the most sensitive area of its body) with any kind of instrument available. If a knife is used, stab at its eyes and gill slits. Use your fist and feet only as a last resort since the shark's abrasive hide will easily tear your skin and possibly cause profuse bleeding. You must now become the aggressor in an attempt to frighten him off.

8. If you are caught in a sea disaster, keep your clothing and shoes on for protection against sharkskin lacerations. Stay close to the group of survivors. If a shark attack is imminent, form a tight circle and face outward keeping the shark in view at all times. Be prepared to repel an attack using your fists or feet if no striking object is available.

9. If you are seized by a shark, cry for help and muster all your strength to fight him off. This is the critical moment when you must try to think clearly. Bang his snout, gouge his eyes, kick, yell—anything so that he will release his hold upon you.

10. If you are injured and the attack is terminated, the bleeding can regain the shark's attention immediately and, if possible, should be controlled to avoid shock even before reaching shore. Depending upon the extent of the injury, first aid or hospitalization should be sought immediately.

11. Be sensible and treat all sharks as they really are—untamed

wild animals that should be considered potentially dangerous. Discourage any desire for thrill and bravado.

According to the official shark-attack records, only 27 species have been singled out as definite menaces to man. This number could be much greater since many unidentified species have been implicated in both inshore and offshore attacks. In the aftermath of many air and sea disasters, several oceanic species have never been identified. In many cases, no clues were discovered and reports from eye-witnesses were vague, making positive identification impossible.

In one study of over 1,000 case histories of shark attacks made throughout the world, only 40 of these were positively identified. This hampers the researchers conducting experiments to determine the feasibility of a specific repellent or deterrent.

Many species of sharks can be identified by the shape of their teeth.

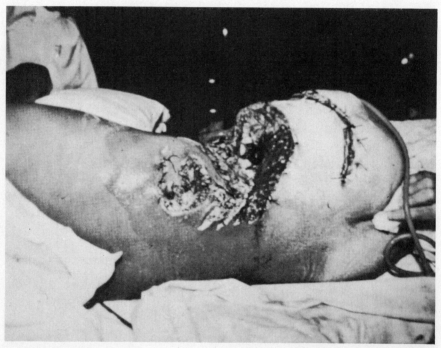

A South African shark-attack victim. This 16-year-old male's injuries included wounds on arms, legs, and right flank that resulted in the perforation of the small and large bowels, the exposure of a kidney and hip bone, and the removal of most of the right gluteal muscles. A seven-foot ragged tooth shark weighing at least 200 pounds is suspected of being responsible for the attack. (Courtesy Oceanographic Research Institute, Durban, South Africa; Journal of the Royal Naval Medical Service)

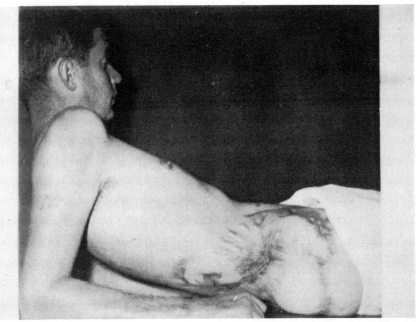

Four months later, the victim is fully recovered in spite of the severity of his wounds that healed extremely well without the need for skin grafting. The victim was fortunate and owes his life to effective emergency treatment and surgical skill. (Courtesy Oceanographic Research Institute, Durban South Africa; Journal of the Royal Naval Medical Service)

However, there are so many species whose teeth bear a close resemblance that positive identification is practically impossible by this method alone. Sometimes a shark can be identified by the nature of the wounds inflicted upon a victim, especially if tooth fragments have broken off in the wounds; a common occurrence in serious attacks. Many marine laboratories have a permanent collection of shark jaws representing the species common to their area. This helps to identify a species when a local attack occurs. Sometimes a wound can be duplicated by closing these laboratory jaws onto a soft material such as modeling clay to simulate an actual shark bite. When compared to the actual wound, the impression in the material could help establish the shark's identity.

Not all species of sharks bite in the same way. Some can sever their prey with one bite since their teeth are constructed for cutting action. Another may grasp and tear at its vicims, shaking its entire body in the process of ripping the flesh apart. In many species, the shape of the teeth in the lower jaw is slightly different from those of the upper jaw making identification difficult if not impossible when only one tooth or fragment is available for study.

Shark-attack victim, male, age 10. Almost 1,000 stitches were required to close wounds on hands, arms, legs, feet, and buttocks after he was attacked 4 times by a nine-foot silky shark in five feet of water along one of central Florida's east coast beaches. (Courtesy Morris M. Vorenberg)

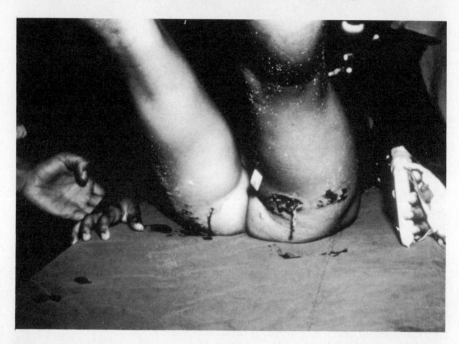

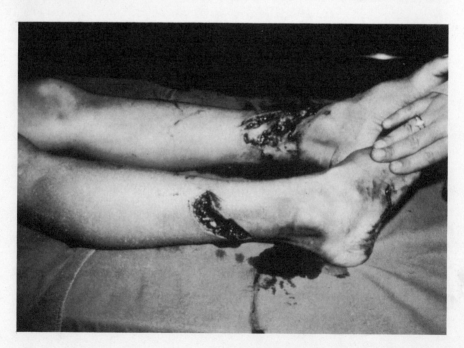

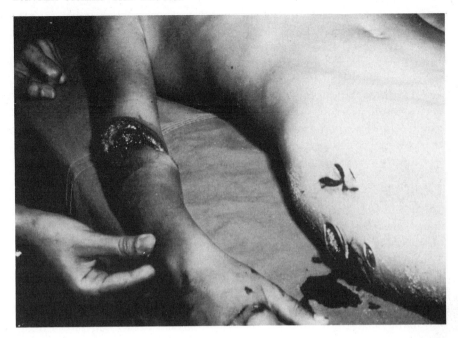

At the beginning of World War II when news of mass shark attacks upon survivors reached servicemen, the psychological impact was paralyzing. The morale of Allied naval and air-force personnel dipped drastically. The U.S. Office of Scientific Research and Development promptly initiated an all-out effort to discover an effective method to protect victims of air and sea disasters against sharks.

Some of the world's ranking marine biologists were assembled to determine why sharks attack people and if ways could be found to discourage them. Scientists worked around the clock, conducting countless experiments. Scores of chemists and experienced divers ran many tests with dyes, chemicals, and assorted electronic devices designed to repel or deter sharks. Serious problems arose in trying to conduct experiments under both natural and artificial conditions. In some cases, the open ocean served as a testing ground and sharks were hard to find. Some species of sharks reacted to repellents; others were unaffected. Weather, visibility, and water temperature were only a few of the factors involved in conducting accurate experiments. Sometimes a repellent wouldn't work under all weather conditions. At other times, the repellent was effective on certain species only. Most repellents failed to discourage many of the larger sharks, especially the man-eating kinds. The problem was complex and exasperating. Scientists were confounded and began to realize how little they knew about one of the oldest predators on earth. No repellent was found to be a hun-

dred percent effective, but some repellents were eventually accepted that provided additional safeguard measures for survivors.

As a result of these early experiments, a little more was learned
about the peculiar personalities of various species of sharks. To bolster
the sagging morale of service personnel, survival booklets containing
cartoons illustrating the dos and don'ts of antishark warfare were issued to those who might come in contact with sharks. The shark was
ridiculed and its potential threat debunked. Psychologically, the booklet was a success—except for those who found themselves confronted
by hungry sharks in the water. But, as the experiments continued,
shark lore was increasing and the survival booklet was revised with a
more realistic approach.

Ship-sinkings account for the greatest number of mass attacks by
sharks. During World War II, thousands of ships were sunk and
countless numbers of service men, who managed to escape injury from
explosions or drowning, were brutally attacked or killed by sharks
before they could be rescued. Records are vague as to the number of
fatalities but, according to the many eye-witness reports, the figure
must be staggering.

One of the largest and most tragic mass attacks occurred during
World War II after the *Nova Scotia*, a British troopship, was torpedoed by a German submarine 30 miles off the coast of South Africa
on November 28, 1942.

The *Nova Scotia* was carrying 900 men, 765 of whom were Italian
prisoners of war being transported to a British stockade in Durban.
When the *Nova Scotia* was hit, explosions followed and many men
were injured or killed before they could abandon ship. Lifeboats were
burned or destroyed, forcing the remaining men to jump into the
water wearing only life belts. Of the 900 men, only 192 survived the
sinking and attacking sharks. One survivor, George Kennaugh, a pris-
oner guard, gave the following account of the tragic disaster to the
late Dr. David H. Davies of Durban, South Africa, and a leading
authority on sharks:

> There were hundreds of men around me in the water, swimming and
> clinging to bits of wreckage and rafts. Another South African swam over
> and clung to the oar. He was wearing a life jacket. The two of us drifted
> on a strong current until next morning. . . .
> When it became light my companion said it was better to die than to
> go on holding on like this. He said he was going to let go and refused to
> listen when I told him not to give up. So I asked him to leave me his life
> jacket.
> As he was loosening his life jacket he suddenly screamed and the upper
> part of his body rose out of the water. He fell back and I saw the water
> had become red with blood and that his feet had been bitten off. At this
> moment I saw the gray form of a shark swimming excitedly around and
> I paddled away as fast as I could . Then a number of sharks congregated

around me—I estimated their lengths at between six and seven feet. Every now and then one would come straight for me—I splashed hard and this seemed to drive them away.

I spotted a raft with Italian prisoners, members of the crew of the *Nova Scotia* and a South African sergeant on board—I climbed on board. A locker on the raft contained water and food which saved our lives. Sharks circled continuously and we hit them with spars to keep them away.

Sixty-seven hours after our ship was torpedoed we were rescued by the Portuguese sloop the *Alfonso du Albuquergue*.

During the rescue operations, the Portuguese sailors had to beat off the sharks that were still swimming among the men, rafts, and wreckage. Many victims were found bobbing in the water clad in their life belts minus their legs.

The number of people killed or injured by shark attacks in the aftermath of a major sea disaster can never be determined. Injuries sustained by survivors are often aggravated by sharks, resulting in fatal consequences. Many survivors who were lucky to escape injury become unfortunate victims of shark attacks even after many days adrift. The list of casualties is incredibly long and the number of fatalities caused by sharks alone cannot be verified.

Another example of a major mass attack by sharks was made upon the men of the U.S.S. *Indianapolis*. The bloody slaughter lasted almost five days and five nights.

After completing its secret mission across the Pacific to deliver the atomic bomb that was later dropped on Hiroshima, the *Indianapolis* was torpedoed and sunk by a Japanese submarine on June 29, 1945. The great cruiser shuddered and went to the bottom rapidly, allowing no time for her crew to take to the lifeboats. On the 1,200 men in her crew, about 900 managed to escape from the sinking ship but were helpless—floating in their life jackets. Immediate rescue was not possible since radio silence was enforced to the end. The mission was still secret.

Within hours after the sinking, sharks appeared and began their attacks upon the struggling survivors. Many of the men, knowing that there was a certain amount of safety in numbers, formed groups to discourage the sharks. Still the water turned red as the marauders singled out their victims.

Many died from exhaustion and shock, some of thirst, while others, becoming delirious and tired of the nightmarish horror going on around them day and night, sacrificed themselves to the attackers. The sea-wolves were always present and continued their merciless assaults. Finally, after five days and nights of fighting sharks, the remaining survivors were spotted by aircraft and were soon rescued by a destroyer. Of the 900 men who were able to abandon ship, only 315 survived.

Although the mass attacks made upon the crews of the *Nova Scotia* and the U.S.S. *Indianapolis* are only two accounts of the many major sea disasters that took place during the war, there were hundreds of other ships and aircraft that sank, leaving thousands of men at the mercy of hungry sharks.

The number of air and sea disasters that take place during peace-time is considerably less but sharks will always continue to be a menace to anyone adrift in the open sea.

When little was known about sharks and their behavior, the development of repellents and deterrents was slow. The history of their development is a confused chronicle representing many painstaking, elaborate experiments. Because of the frequent attacks made upon air and sea disaster victims after the beginning of World War II the U.S. Navy inaugurated a crash program to find an effective method to reduce the growing number of attacks. Scientists worked day and night—testing all kinds of substances such as chemical irritants, ink clouds, poison gases, stink bombs, and electronic devices—in an attempt to discourage the murderous instincts of sharks. Over 70 different substances and contrivances were patiently tested by the tedious procedure of trial and error. It was frustrating and discouraging to accept the fact that modern science was unable to develop satisfactory anti-shark measures while fighting men survived the war only to be murdered by another alien enemy.

Finally, before the close of the war, scientists came up with a repellent that had some merit. Called Shark Chaser, it was a combination of repellent and deterrent in one. A standard six-and-one-half-ounce cake of Shark Chaser, consisting of 20 percent copper acetate and 80 percent nigrosine dye mixed with carbo-wax, would last up to four hours. The copper acetate simulated the odor of decomposed shark flesh, which was found to be obnoxious to a shark's sense of smell. The nigrosine dye (highly soluble in water) resembles the inky smoke screen created by squid and octopi when they attempt to shield themselves from predators.

Although Shark Chaser was not nearly 100 percent effective, it did offer some measure of safety and did wonders for service personnel by providing a psychological crutch in relieving their fears. Since the development of Shark Chaser, scientists are still searching for a better repellent or device that will discourage *all* species of sharks under any condition. Today, Shark Chaser is still part of the standard survival equipment of some service personnel and, in some instances, is used commercially by the public.

To increase the safety of swimmers, divers, and air-sea disaster survivors, research studies are continually being conducted in large laboratories all over the world. Although the expense involved in capturing and maintaining them in captivity (to test repellents or deterrent devices) is prohibitive, the vital problem is keeping them alive long enough under conditions that will provide reasonably conclusive results. Unfortunately, many offshore pelagic species (such as the white tip oceanic sharks, makos, and great whites), which are responsible for a great number of attacks, do not survive in captivity long enough to make attack studies practical. Consequently, in order to develop effective countermeasures against attack, further research must also continue into the shark's physiology, behavior, and ecology so that the problem of maintaining them in captivity can be solved.

While the search for effective antishark measures continues, some scientists specialize in experiments dealing with ways to deter sharks electronically.

After intensive studies were made on various species of sharks and their olfactory and sensory organs, scientists discovered that all sharks do not react in the same way to repellents. Some species *were* repelled, while others were attracted.

In experiments dealing with the sharks' efficient sensory organs such as the lateris system, tests were conducted with the use of electronic equipment to search for a sound frequency that might repel or deter them. Even music was employed in some of the experiments—without success. Rock 'n' roll made them nervous and hyperactive; selections from the classics, on the other hand, seemed to calm them and, in some cases, created a trancelike condition. But this, in no way, deterred their curiosity or reduced a potential threat.

Currently, a new study is being instituted by U.S. Navy scientists who have recorded the sounds made by killer whales. Amplified recordings of their shrill screams have been hurled into the paths of migrating gray whales. The experiment, which involved over 100 gray whales, proved that the sounds of the killer whale will frighten them and cause them to flee.

These eerie screams are high-pitched sounds that often change in frequency. Even sea lions run for their lives when they hear the recordings. The success of a shark deterrent such as this will be realized *only* if all the species of sharks that are known to be dangerous to man are effected sufficiently to discourage an attack.

Since the killer whale is known as one of the shark's natural enemies, scientists are optimistic about the possibility of using the recorded sounds of killer whales to deter sharks. Further tests and methods are presently being conducted by the U.S. Naval Undersea Research and Development Center.

Other experiments dealing with the visual acuteness of sharks revealed that they are not as color-blind as suspected. There is mounting evidence that sharks are attracted by the brightness or color of an object. Although their sight is greatly limited when it comes to detail, their ability to distinguish objects at a distance in cloudy water is good.

In recent tests conducted by research scientists, a dummy of a child in a yellow life jacket was attacked repeatedly by sharks while the dummies in red or black life jackets escaped undamaged. Conclusive evidence was established that the bright-yellow life jackets, which assist rescuers to find survivors at sea, can also attract man-eating sharks. This knowledge creates an impasse. It is more practical for a survivor to take his chances with a yellow life jacket that will attract sharks or should he wear a dark jacket that reduces his chances for rescue?

Perhaps one of the most practical and effective means of protecting air-sea disaster survivors against a shark attack is a simple plastic sack. The sack, called the Johnson Shark Screen by the U.S. Navy, was developed by D. C. Scott Johnson of the Naval Undersea Warfare Center, San Diego, California. Dr. Johnson and his associates conducted extensive tests—subjecting themselves and the Shark Screen to many man-eating sharks—in order to determine its effectiveness. All tests were successful, proving conclusively that sharks exhibited little or no interest in the Shark Screen, or were unaware of its human contents.

The Johnson Shark Screen is a black, plastic, water-filled bag, six feet long and supported by three yellow floatation rings. Its occupant floats freely inside the bag while the brightly colored supporting rings serve as a prominent object for visual detection by searching aircraft or vessels. The bag also helps to retain some of the survivor's body heat and, when not used in this respect, can serve as poncho, stretcher, sleeping bag or a fresh-water collector. Uninflated, the bag is light and durable and is part of the standard survival gear attached to the life jacket.

As the name implies, the Shark Screen is a device that "screens out" any visual or odoriferous attraction that might stimulate a shark's attention. The screen is a visual deterrent rather than a repellent, providing its occupant with a true camouflage.

Another concept in preventing shark attacks has recently been expounded by Captain David Baldridge, a U.S. Navy scientist who conducts antishark experiments at the Mote Marine Laboratory in Sarasota, Florida.

After making an exhaustive study of the weight and balance properties of a shark, Captain Baldridge is convinced that the most effective way of incapacitating a shark is to disturb its weight and balance system.

Since sharks are slightly heavier than water, they will sink if they stop swimming. A shark's critical balance is maintained by oil in its enormous liver. As a result of his hydrodynamic studies, Captain Baldridge suggests that a small gas bubble injected into the shark would hamper its maneuverability and natural swimming abilities, making it unable to execute an attack. A simple defense weapon could be devised that would serve as part of the standard survival gear presently issued to service personnel.

A new antishark weapon such as the one described was recently developed by the scientists at the Naval Undersea Research and Development Center. The weapon, when fired, shoots a dart that injects carbon dioxide gas into the shark. The Apollo 15 astronauts wore these weapons as part of their survival gear when they splashed down in the Pacific on their return trip from the moon. This new idea for preventing shark attacks appears to be one of the more realistic methods of dealing with the problem and shows great promise for the future protection of survivors in the open sea.

For the protection of swimmers along shark-inhabited beaches, other antishark attack measures must be employed to reduce the menace. So far, concentrated line-fishing for sharks in some areas has proven successful in removing the growing threat.

It is common knowledge that the hammerhead, dusky, tiger, and the lemon sharks are constant threats to swimmers along Florida's Gold Coast. The complete elimination of these dangerous species can never be accomplished. However, if the life of only one person is saved by angling methods, then the entire program is more than worthwhile. In one particular instance, angling methods were so successful in reducing the local shark population that the technique was endorsed by one of our country's foremost authorities on sharks who said, "The Palm Beach Sharkers have given their community about $100,000 worth of free protection every year."

Ironically, some marine communities along Florida's Gold Coast were indifferent while others were actually infuriated with the shark-fishing along their shores, since it revealed to the resort trade that sharks were numerous in local waters. This supposedly created a scare among the Gold Coast vacationists with a resulting scarcity of tourist dollars. Controversy waged between the pro and con factions of each municipality. Finally, in some communities, legislation was passed and ordinances enforced that prohibited shark-fishing. Even today, in some areas, shark-fishing is strictly forbidden. This put unfair pressure on organizations such as the Palm Beach Sharkers forcing them to fish elsewhere.

However, in other areas along the coast, shark fishermen are welcome—the more the merrier—for those city fathers believe that any kind of strategy to help prevent shark attacks is good, not only for their own citizens but also for the visiting tourists who share their beaches. These municipalities accept the fact that their inshore waters do contain a frightening number of sharks and agree that the best way to reduce the menace is to inaugurate a concentrated fishing effort. The idea of simple hook-and-line methods was proven successful long ago and is still in actual practice. In fact, this method is still in use in such areas as Hawaii, the South Seas, Africa and Australia, where attacks in the past have been most prevalent.

Up to this time no mechanical or electronic devices have been successful in repelling sharks from beach areas. Wire fences or "meshing" is a satisfactory means of keeping sharks away from the bathing areas, but this method requires a large number of heavy-duty nets while maintenance and periodic replacement makes the cost prohibitive. There has been some success with this method on the beaches of Australia and South Africa, but stringing lengthy nets along most shorelines is impractical because of the character of the beach terrain.

As man becomes more aware of the rape and contamination taking place in his immediate environment now, more than ever, he will be forced to turn to the sea—that vast and practically untapped resource of plants, animals and minerals—in search of the requirements necessary for his survival on earth. Regardless of his attempts to preserve his environment, if he does not look to the sea for sustenance he can still perish. His population is increasing at an alarming rate and, in order for him to maintain life on a comfortable level, he must enter the sea with his tools of science and technology.

Divers, armed with these tools are already plunging into the depths on exploratory missions to evaluate the valuable natural resources that nature provided for its creatures. Man will study and analyze the ocean's secrets and pioneer agricultural methods using the ocean bottom as a farm land. He will even have to modify his terrestrial architectural structures and anchor them to the floor of the ocean where they will become self-contained communities.

The ocean covers about 71 percent of the earth's surface. It consists of an intricate society of thousands upon thousands of marine creatures living and dying, balanced by nature's strict precepts. Many of these creatures have yet to be considered as subjects to provide man with the essentials for his survival. Among these creatures, man will encounter the shark—that mysterious, misunderstood, and potentially dangerous animal that will attempt to block man's entry into its domain.

First, man must find a way to prevent these sea-wolves from prowling about his doorsteps and interrupting his research just as the early land pioneers drove the wild animals of an untamed wilderness from their doors.

6

Man Against Shark

SHARKS AND MAN SHARE MANY COMMON CHARACTERISTICS, BOTH CAN BE hostile, terrifying, mysterious, and unpredictable. In many instances man, too, will even put his life on the line and pursue sharks. Man (always hungry for adventure and excitement) sometimes invades a sharks province—against his better judgment—to satisfy *his* appetite. He may effectuate this strange confrontation for various reasons not clear even to himself; to experience the thrills associated with danger, to enjoy the sport, to feel a sense of accomplishment, or to escape from the norm.

A dramatic duel takes place when he enters their arena and stalks them courageously on their own terms. Man has always been the hunter and the conquest syndrome is clearly displayed when he charges into this weird engagement. Whether he pursues sharks with a spear, knife, powerhead, lasso, hook and line, hypodermic needle, or camera, he achieves a sense of fulfillment, and because his stature is increased by his courage, the limits of his world are expanded.

The underwater cameraman, determined to get a closer shot of his quarry, rests his bulky camera between the widely spaced vertical bars of his aluminum cage. He is nervous and afraid but his hands are steady as they grip the switch that will start the filming never before accomplished, of one of the world's most feared predators—the great white shark in its natural habitat.

Barrels of fresh cow's blood are poured overboard clouding the water surrounding the cage. The thick red dye slowly dissipates as the current begins to break it up into long red trails drifting off into the distance. Suddenly, from the vastness of the deep turquoise depths, a great white appears, cruising suspiciously but boldly just on the fringe of the blood streak. Quickly it picks up the scent and charges swiftly into the blood-stained corridor leading to the cage. Its large

*This 37-foot whale shark was caught by Captain Johnny Cass of Bimini,
Bahamas, using only an anchor line and grapnel. Harmless and docile, whale
sharks are the largest fishlike creatures in the sea and feed only upon small
fish and marine organisms. Bob Straughan, aquarist and author, in foreground.
(Photo by Ralph L. Bowden)*

black eyes roll back, it thrusts its snout upward and its huge mouth
opens baring many ugly teeth as it attempts to seize the quarter of
beef hanging from inside the cage. The cameraman flinches but
squeezes the camera switch quickly to record this macabre scene, the

fearless assault by a 1,000 pound killer shark. The beast crashes headlong into the cage and bites savagely at the bars, twisting them and
breaking off several sharp teeth. It shakes the cage so violently that
the cameraman almost loses his balance. Enraged, the great white
swims a short distance away, circles, and returns for another attack.
The frightened cameraman is badly shaken and crouches down at
the back of the cage. He realizes that the bars twisted open by the
shark's first attack now offers less protection against the bloody-thirsty
predator's second rush. But he keeps the camera running and its lens
expertly trained upon its formidable subject.

The moment of truth had come for shark photographer, Peter
Gimbel. The infernal scene was finally captured on film after spending five months and traveling 12,000 miles over three oceans in search
of the great white shark, one of the most dangerous marine animals
in the ocean.

Why does a man, heir to a department store fortune and a comfortable job on Wall Street, New York, decide to risk his life to take
underwater movies of the world's largest man-eating sharks?

Peter Gimbel has completed one of the finest documentaries on
sharks ever shown. He produced and directed *Blue Water, White
Death*, a successful full-length film that is currently being shown at
leading cinemas throughout the world. Because of its unusual appeal,
many theaters were forced to hold the film over and, in some areas,
box-office records were made.

"It is like every adventure," he states. "Why do people climb moun-
tains? Or explore space? Most everyone has some of the curiosity of
the explorer. One needs or wants to explain his motivations."

Gray haired and distinguished looking, Gimbel, 42, is no novice at
this business of documenting his underwater adventures. In 1956, the
day after the tragic sinking of the *Andrea Dorea* off Nantucket, Massachusetts, Gimbel was the first to photograph the great ship lying on
the bottom in 225 feet of water. It was an exremely hazardous under-
taking. Surrounded by treacherous icy currents and murky water, Gimbel had to utilize all his energy and skills to photograph the funereal
subject that was later published in Life magazine.

Gimbel has always been fascinated by sharks. In 1965 he made a
fine documentary called *In The World of Sharks* about the blue sharks
found in Long Island, New York, waters. His other achievements include the filming of *The Noisy Underwater World of The Weddell
Seal* and *Whale Ho*. Both films were acclaimed as great contributions
to natural science. Because of his considerable knowledge and experience on the subject of skin-diving, he wrote an informative and interesting article for the *Encyclopaedia Britannica*.

Gimbel's film *Blue Water, White Death* differs greatly from Cousteau's famous films. After much research and preparation, Gimbel

succeeded in recording, at great risk to himself and his associates, many actual encounters with the white shark. The film is an authentic production and shows how many varieties of sharks (while in their natural habitat) feed, attack, and react to man. Above all, it portrays the daring characteristics of the most elusive and dangerous shark in the sea. Gimbel's dreams have been realized. The capture of this particular subject on celluloid has become a substantial contribution not only to the entertainment field but to all those who are trying to understand the mysterious ways of the shark.

He was no young fellow, a man somewhere in his early fifties, well built and strong as any young blade his size. He stood erect in his heavy scuba gear and stared out over the majestic calm of the Gulf of Mexico. Somewhere in its quiet green depths, he knew, man-eating sharks were lurking. He also knew that hidden deep in their livers was a substance (squalene) that might save many people from dying of heart failure and a lipid (restim) capable of fighting cancer.

He reached down to make sure the sharp knife was in its sheath and strapped tightly to his leg, not that it would help much but he felt more secure knowing it was available if something . . . He dismissed the thought, turned to his assistants and said, "OK, let's go get 'em!"

Dr. John H. Heller, president and executive director of the New England Institute for Medical Research, is one of America's foremost research scientists in organic chemistry. He will take almost any risk to find a solution to a complex problem in medical research.

In the mid-fifties while studies were being made dealing with the effects of cholesterol in the human body, it was discovered that the livers of certain sharks contained a rare substance called squalene, a fatty material made up of precholesterol molecules. Knowledge gleaned from these studies would be of valuable assistance to specialists in the treatment of heart disease and related disorders. This meant that Dr. Heller and his associates would have to conduct extensive experiments on live sharks—injecting them with radioactive carbon that would find its way into the livers and lated be absorbed in the squalene. After the shark manufactured its squalene, the carbon-tagged molecules could be removed for use in cholesterol experiments with laboratory animals. Many sharks were needed in this work, so the long search began for an area in the ocean where sharks were abundant.

After many months of seeking a suitable site to begin operations, Dr. Heller and his associates were pleased to hear that Dr. Eugenie Clark's newly-opened Cape Haze Marine Laboratory located on Florida's west coast was available. Dr. Clark's facilities were ideal since she was also interested in catching sharks and keeping them alive for her own studies. Dr. Heller's institute and Dr. Clark's laboratory collabo-

Dr. John H. Heller, president of the New England Institute for Medical Research, inspects some of the experimental equipment used to extract the host defense-stimulating agent from shark livers. (Courtesy Lionel Murphy, Sarasota, Florida)

Mini-plant for on-the-spot processing of shark livers at the Cape Haze Marine Laboratory. Four hundred pounds of dry ice were used daily to keep the shark-liver extract at correct temperatures for later experiments at the New England Institute for Medical Research. The chemicals used were so toxic that it was necessary to have an open-air plant to insure adequate ventilation. (Courtesy Lionel Murphy, Sarasota, Florida)

rated and established a convenient affiliation to conduct extensive shark research. The business (scientists hunting for sharks) began.

It soon became apparent that catching sharks was not only a difficult task but a dangerous one as well. Often Dr. Heller had to don his diving equipment to assist in the capture of the writhing creatures. Several times he tried injecting the radioactive carbon on the spot (a hazardous and tricky operation), but most of the time he waited until they were back in port. Usually the sharks were towed slowly and carefully from the longline to the dock.

Some sharks were lively and cantankerous, making them extremely difficult to handle, while others were half-dead and unpredictable after fighting for hours to free themselves from the hooks. When they arrived at the waterfront pens, the weak sharks had to be "walked" to force water through their gills. It was a risky business causing scientists to step with care and spectators to shudder. Those that survived then had to be induced to eat so that they would live at least a week between the injections and the extraction of squalene.

After all the arduous work, the experiments had to be discontinued. Too many sharks died and too little squalene was recovered from the survivors.

A few years later Dr. Heller and his associates discovered that the lipid (fat) in the shark's liver greatly stimulates the body's natural defense in combating viral or nonviral tumors. They called the lipid *restim* after many experiments proved that it did stimulate the reticuloendothelial system known as RES. RES is one of the body's most important defense activities.

Restim has been shown to reduce or delay the occurrence of tumors, slows the growth, slows metastasis (spreading), causes tumors to shrink, and keeps animals with tumors alive longer.

Although many more experiments must be done on animals, and the need to synthesize restim is acute, the prospects of controlling and treating cancer in humans appears optimistic. In addition, there is hope of developing an opposite agent that will inhibit the RES from rejecting organ transplants.

Dr. Heller and his associates returned to Cape Haze and, with the active assistance of Dr. Clark, began another shark-hunting expedition. This time the going was a little easier since injecting squirming man-eaters was unnecessary. All Dr. Heller required was a lot of live sharks—the larger the better (unfortunately, more dangerous!)—to sacrifice for their livers. But the livers had to be extremely fresh before the complicated process of lipid extraction began. Since the lipid loses its potency within 15 minutes after a shark's death, dockside facilities were set up for the slaughter.

These men of science worked hard while enduring many hardships and disappointments. They risked serious injury to capture such fero-

Equipped with scuba gear, a research scientist tows live sharks (just removed from the longline) to the boat. (Courtesy Medical World News)

cious "laboratory animals" and the production of restim was painfully small. Still, they paved the way for future studies that will certainly benefit mankind. Detailed analyses of the shark's lipid will surely lead to the production of a powerful synthetic compound in the future.

So, dear reader, if you hate sharks and dread swimming in shark-infested waters, take every precaution but don't judge them too harshly. Try instead to show a little tolerance for their existence. The shark that you might see may be the one that could save your life!

Most people find sharks highly repulsive even if they aren't afraid of them. Some few people respect sharks as subjects for scientific research. But for Gerrit Klay, collector and majordomo of Shark-Quarium, Grassy Key, Florida, sharks have a special meaning. His attachment for them borders upon genuine affection.

Klay has a maternal fondness for these creatures and thinks nothing of spending an entire night with a sick or ill-natured shark that might be having difficulty adjusting to its new surroundings.

This stern-looking but mild-mannered man, whose clipped sentences retain a slight Dutch accent, abhors the reckless destruction of the marine environment and considers it sacrilegious to kill sharks wantonly unless it is in the interests of medical research.

"These wild animals are born to function in nature's scheme of things," Klay firmly states, "and their annihilation would certainly upset her well-designed plan."

Klay is a modern version of "bring 'em back alive" Frank Buck, whose popularity began in the forties. Buck was the famous "white hunter" who captured wild animals alive in countries all over the world for distribution to zoos and public attractions. His fame gained momentum when Hollywood documented his hazardous occupation on film and later serialized his many action-packed adventures.

Although Klay is not a celebrity in the Buck tradition, he too stalks wild animals, traps them, and "brings 'em back alive." His quarries are various species of sharks ranging from the docile nurse to the formidable man-eating tiger. Then he ships them alive to aquariums and marine attractions throughout the world. The potential danger in capturing these sharks could equal that of hunting the dangerous wild lions in Africa or the man-eating Bengal tigers!

Gerrit Klay (left), director of Shark-Quarium in Grassy Key, Florida, and assistant transfer a small bonnet shark from "corral" to shipping container.

Klay is a fearless man, the kind usually found among that select fraternity of wild-animal trainers and hunters. He respects sharks and is fully aware of the risks involved in handling these man-eaters. He has a compassion for what he always refers to as his "animals"—a genuine fondness that most people might find hard to understand. Strangely enough the sharks seem to sense this devotion and seldom give him any real trouble.

Klay is philosophical about shark attacks. After handling thousands of sharks he is unable to exhibit any scars that result from his occupation.

"Except for a little nip here and there or an occasional leg bruise, I guess I've been pretty lucky" he declares. "I suppose some day I'll really get a good bite. But I wouldn't hold any grudge against the animal. Heck, some people have been attacked who've never even seen a shark!"

Three years ago, after leaving a prestigious job as head aquarist of the Cleveland Aquarium, Klay plunged headlong into the field of collecting sharks and studying methods of keeping them alive in captivity. Because of his close association with his "animals," he is probably one of the most knowledgeable fellows around. Known as the "shark-man" by the local citizenry, he is a gracious host to any visitors who wish to inspect the facilities he proudly calls Shark-Quarium. Even those who come only to gawk at the many sharks swimming in lazy circles in the tank and seagoing "corrals" that make up his fenced-in waterfront stockade are welcome.

Shark-Quarium is an unpretentious complex originally built by Klay as an experimental station. It is located on the shores of Grassy Key in the central part of the Florida Keys that make up the southern out islands of the United States. The location is ideal since many species of shark roam these waters.

Some of the facilities at Shark-Quarium consist of several above-ground tanks used for exhibitions and experimental purposes. Large steel chain-linked fences make up the holding pens along the waterfront. Klay uses these to store the larger sharks prior to a shipment.

As Klay became better known in this highly specialized work, countless numbers of scientists and marine directors, intrigued with his methods of shark survival, began beating a path to his door. This soon necessitated the installation of a laboratory and study room for visiting scientists who prefer to conduct special research studies privately. He even provided housing so that they could carry out around-the-clock experiments.

Because of Klay's unusual attachment for his sharks, he will often stand an all-night vigil over a sick or badly adjusted shark. It is easy to detect the affection that he holds for these critters; it is a sincere regard that is based not upon their monetary value (he can catch all he wants) but upon scientific curiosity.

Whenever inclement weather threatens the well-being of his sharks, his real nightmare begins. Drastic changes in weather can force him to watch over his charges day and night until the weather subsides. Sudden cold snaps may reduce water temperatures low enough to threaten a shark's survival or perhaps cause death.

On one particular winter night, a cold nor'wester blew over the Florida Keys and was followed by a three-day cold spell that broke all weather bureau records. The sudden chill killed countless fish of many species. For three day and three nights, Klay had to maintain a water-temperature watch, transferring his shallow-water species into tanks containing warmer water to save them from dying. Strong winds and heavy seas buffeted and slammed into Klay's holding pens—opening holes large enough for some of his sharks to escape. On several occasions during the night, risking penumonia and attack, he was forced to wade among the nervous sharks and repair the damage. When the temperature finally returned to normal, a completely exhausted "shark-man" fell into bed minus 20 pounds.

Before Klay developed his successful technique of jetting a plane-load of live sharks to public aquariums throughout the United States and Europe, some experts were skeptical and called his shark-lift a real "mission impossible." To prove his theories and confound his critics, Klay designed and built an unique and practical shipping container that provides a complete life-support system for sharks of all sizes. In effect, it is a large coffinlike fiberglassed box outfitted with a battery-operated oxygen system. He devised a special kind of mouthpiece which, when placed on the shark's mouth, serves as a kind of offbeat scuba gear. The water that flows from this device is forced through the shark's gills with a high concentration of oxygen supplied by a portable bottle installed in the container.

To insure the safe arrival of his charges, Klay must always accompany them on their flights. During these trips he supplements his life-support system by exercising and massaging his air-sick sharks periodically within the containers to stimulate their sluggish circulation. Some of his sharks are man-eaters weighing as much as 400 pounds. Exercising them is a most unenviable (if not hazardous) chore!

When the heart-chilling cry of *shark attack!* shatters the air of Palm Beach County, Florida, Morris Vorenberg immediately drops whatever he's doing (unless he's fighting a big shark!) and, like a professional detective in hot pursuit of a killer, goes swiftly to the scene. There he begins a thorough investigation of the circumstances surrounding the tragic incident. No one can deny that a unprovoked shark attack is a direct and murderous assault upon man.

*Live sharks in their special containers are loaded on jet aircraft and trans-
ported to aquariums throughout the United States and Europe.*

If a monster shark (sometimes they measure 12 to 15 feet) is sighted
in the area, Vorenberg is notified. He gathers up his fishing gear,
alerts his club members and they charge out to destroy a potential
killer of swimmers.

He has documentary evidence of many shark attacks upon people,
but these cases rarely appear in print. Either the newspapers weren't
informed of the incidents or the news was suppressed by municipal
officials afraid that bad publicity would drive the tourists away.

Despite the lack of civic cooperation, Vorenberg (he is really gung
ho on the subject) continues his private war on sharks, and sometimes
people! He advocates continual, concentrated hook-and-line fishing
pressure along the beaches in order to reduce the shark menace. Some
of our country's leading shark authorities endorse his idea whole-
heartedly and many of the local citizens regard him as an unsung
hero in the fight for safety. Others simply shake their heads and are
content to "let sleeping sharks lie" in the interests of the tourist
dollar.

Vorenberg is undoubtedly the sharkiest man in the county. He has
made an exhaustive study of sharks, having spent some 20 years dili-

gently fishing for the critters. During this time he became an expert, dedicated naturalist, keeping flawless records of his catches and observations. Some of his statistics have become priceless to scientific research and important studies related to sharks. In cooperation with a government tagging program for the purpose of migratory studies, Vorenberg personally tagged over 500 sharks during a three-year period. Once he caught one of his own tagged sharks—four months later and 35 miles from the initial tagging location.

As an active consultant for the Shark Research Panel of the American Institute of Biological Sciences and a representative of the Smithsonian Institute, Vorenberg is often called upon to speak before civic organizations. He welcomes every opportunity to speak to those who might have mixed emotions about the large shark population in their waters. His views and constructive suggestions have been noted several times in the newspapers.

In addition to writing two interesting books, *What About Sharks?* and *Shark Tales,* he also composed a highly informative and scientific report called "The Cannibalistic Tendencies of Lemon and Bull Sharks," which was published in *COPEIA* July 20, 1962. He is currently conducting a research project dealing with fetal counts to determine the sex ratio of sharks. After dissecting several thousand gravid females, he counted 11 thousand unborn sharks, arriving at a sex ratio of 59-6% females and 40.4% males. The figures so far cover 14 different species.

At present, Vorenberg is spearheading plans for the organization of a Florida Shark Fishing Association, which would bring all local clubs under the rules, regulations, and bylaws of the state association. When any group—anywhere in Florida—desires help in establishing a club, Vorenberg and his co-workers are happy to assist them. So far he has been instrumental in the formation of four clubs in the state.

The underlying objective of the association is to embark upon a public relations and educational program to dispel much of the existing misconceptions that people have about sharks and to help overcome some of the antipathy that local communities have shown toward the shark fishermen.

Vorenberg expresses it well when he says, "The association would be a means of control over the individual angler and/or club toward eliminating one of the main gripes . . . that shark carcasses are left on the beach and/or that the fishermen leave the beaches in an unsightly condition. Another complaint that could be overcome through the association and its control over members is the one that shark anglers interfere with other fishermen and/or if fishing from a beach, bathers and swimmers. On the educational side—shark fishing does not attract sharks from far distant areas; shark fishing does reduce the resident shark population, adverse publicity associated with the presence of sharks can be turned in favor of the community permitting shark fishing."

Vorenberg's intense interest in sharks began about 20 years ago. At that time he was a fisherman with only a casual interest in sharks, catching one now and then unintentionally. One day, from curiosity, he dissected a large shark to examine its stomach contents and discovered what appeared to be the remains of human bones. The incident was electrifying and he soon developed a desire for further knowledge about these man-eating creatures. He began fishing for them with a fervent compulsion for sport and inquiry. Meanwhile, he contacted shark experts and absorbed everything written on the subject.

During his many years of sharking and data collecting, Vorenberg has been attacked by sharks, bitten on two different occasions, and involved in a boat attack while tagging one. None of these incidents have deterred him or created thoughts of quitting his dangerous avocation. Actually, they merely fired his enthusiasm for further association with the beasts. Morris Vorenberg is a naturalist and this is his way of doing his "thing" for the benefit of mankind.

Sharks have an extraordinary effect upon some people. Sometimes they become victims of a publicity stunt to satisfy someone's quixotic dreams.

What motivates a 62-year-old concert violinist to swim 100 miles from Key West, Florida, to Bimini, Bahamas—with a homemade craft especially rigged to use a dangerous shark for propulsion?

Paul Chotteau was consumed by this challenge without knowing exactly why, except that he wanted to be the first to accomplish this bold and unusual feat.

Chotteau's past life had been colorful and even dangerous at times. Born in France in 1898, he studied music and graduated from the famous Paris Conservatory of Music. When World War I broke out he joined the French Air Force and was awarded the Croix de Guerre for heroism. He came to America in 1929 and played violin under the famous Walter Damrosch, conductor of the New York Symphony Orchestra. This was followed by an engagement as concertmaster of New York's Criterion Theater.

He always enjoyed swimming and had no fear of ocean or sharks. His passion for endurance swimming was recognized officially in 1936 when he completed the longest ocean swim ever recorded—50 miles from Santa Barbara to near Venice, California. In 1940, when he was 42 years old, he broke his own record and established a new one that still stands—114 miles from Bimini, Bahamas, almost to West Palm Beach, Florida.

For many years Chotteau dreamed of a device that could employ a shark to pull him along on an extended swimming expedition. In 1945 he began designing a craft that would satisfy his concept of shark propulsion. Meanwhile, he became so engrossed with his project that he wrote a book entitled *Oscar*, the story of an old man who dreamed of going to sea in a boat pulled by a shark called Oscar.

Without help of any kind, Chotteau finally completed his home-made craft in 1960 and began preparations for catching and harnessing a shark suitable for his long journey. His craft *The Spirit of Betty*, named after his dead wife, was a weird-looking contraption indeed but neatly constructed. It consisted of two pontoons separated by a framework that held a special rig for harnessing a shark. Chotteau was pulled behind the craft, steering it with lines attached to the rudders mounted on each pontoon. Strangely enough, it worked successfully over short distances but his "motor" frequently conked out on long trips.

Although sharks basically are rugged creatures, special care must be taken to keep them alive. In most cases they soon die from mishandling or the inability to adjust to captivity. Chotteau's biggest problem was obtaining enough "motors" and keeping them running. These big sea-going engines were hard to find and, when caught, were usually half-dead or refused to provide Chotteau with the required horse-power. In addition, the element of danger was always present since he needed at least a 10- or 12-foot shark to serve as his power plant. Unfortunately, the only available "motors" of this size in Key West waters were tiger sharks, celebrated for their man-eating tendencies!

Chotteau enlisted the help of several Key West fishermen who respected him for his courage and past achievements. They became intrigued with his project when they were convinced that he was serious. During the course of a year many sharks were caught and Chotteau made several attempts to reach Bimini. Several times newspaper headlines heralded his courageous spirit. Unfortunately, all his attempts ended in failure. The sharks simply refused to become man-driven engines! Chotteau's dream collapsed, the publicity died, and he was relegated to that unvictorious but courageous fraternity of forgotten men.

To the thousands who read her book and to everyone who is interested in sharks, the words *Clark* and *shark* are synonymous. Dr. Eugenie Clark began her intimate association with the man-eaters shortly after she organized the Cape Haze Marine Laboratory (now the Mote Marine Laboratory of Sarasota) on Florida's west coast in 1955. While serving as its director for ten years, she conducted a great number of shark experiments in addition to her other studies of marine life. She also assisted the many scientists who came from all parts of the world to carry out experiments relative to their particular fields of research. An ample supply of sharks were caught and kept alive in the large sea pens at the Laboratory waterfront.

When word got around that Eugenie always had plenty of sharks in her "corrals," a steady stream of endocrinologists, physiologists, and parasitologists, eager to experiment with her live subjects, began to storm her unique facilities.

Some of the research requiring the use of live sharks dealt with their respiratory systems, locomotion, visual acuteness, and blood. Others involved using their livers, hormones, glands, and intestines in the interest of medical science. Even shark repellents were tested under the direction of the U.S. Navy Shark Research Group.

Sharks have always been difficult to keep alive in captivity. Soon, Dr. Clark and her assistants were setting out lines with as many as 100 baited hooks to insure an adequate supply for the scientists.

Experts have always considered sharks color-blind until Dr. Clark's tests for color and visual discriminations proved differently. Her experiments disclosed that the senses of sharks are far better developed than originally presumed.

For example, during the course of one and a half years, Dr. Clark conducted periodic experiments with live sharks in a large tank. She actually trained them to work for their dinner by nudging an underwater device which, in turn, rang a bell. Food was rewarded for doing this correctly. This mechanism, when lowered into the water, served as a target for the sharks. The background was formed by a white board that could be changed to one of another color.

The sharks became accustomed to color and gradually developed routine eating habits by favoring these colors. When they bumped the color board food was lowered to them.

One day, to test a shark's color perception and behavioral adjustability, Dr. Clark substituted a color that the shark had never seen before. As the shark approached the target, it stopped short, backed off, and refused to nudge the board or take any food. After the initial shock it developed a kind of neurotic personality as a result of the change in its training routine. From that day on it refused food and soon died of starvation.

"This incident," declares Dr. Clark, "and other experiments that followed, lead one to suspect that sharks are more delicately balanced than we thought."

Although her tests of many shark repellents were not conclusive, Dr. Clark ventures a theory that, by disturbing their natural routine habits, an effective method could be devised in the future that would repel sharks when man invades their natural habitat.

In the past, Dr. Clark has handled thousands of live sharks, many of them extremely dangerous, and has not lost one drop of blood. She did, however, lose blood to a very dead shark. One day, while driving

Dr. Eugenie Clark, ichthyologist, is well known for her many experiments with sharks. Dr. Clark often uses scuba gear in her research studies. (Photo by William Stephens)

to give a lecture, she had to make a sudden stop for a red light. To prevent her exhibits from tumbling to the floor, she reached out and accidentally grazed her arm on the sharp teeth of one of the mounted shark jaws!

In the field of the marine sciences, she is highly respected for her achievements especially in her work with live sharks. Her contributions have opened the way for further important studies with other scientists. In addition to her many papers and articles, Dr. Clark has written two books describing her adventures, which entrance readers of all ages. Both have become popular sellers.

Her first book, *Lady With A Spear*, was published in 1953. A lively book, it tells of her marine research and skin-diving adventures in the Red Sea and the islands of the South Pacific.

Her second book, *The Lady And The Sharks*, in 1969 gives the story of her scientific life and personal adventures during the ten years she directed The Cape Haze Marine Laboratory.

The fascinating accounts of her experiments have stimulated the interest of many people. Her writing could be compared to the impressionable works of Horatio Alger, whose success stories have inspired countless numbers of youngsters. Probably no one in her field has done more than Dr. Clark to influence young people to study ichthyology and related marine biological subjects. She is currently associate professor of Zoology at the University of Maryland. Her classroom students are awed by this tiny and attractive shark tamer.

Now that people are more aware of the severe changes taking place in our ecology because of pollution, they are finding that the marine sciences more than ever play an all-important role in the preservation of our environment.

So, in the classroom might lie Dr. Eugenie Clark's greatest contribution to mankind. The enthusiasm that she generates for the marine sciences infects her students. Known as the "shark lady," she has become the idol and revered heroine of many who want to devote their lives to this important subject.

One of the greatest shark hunters of all time was Captain William E. Young. Known as *Kane Mano*, The Shark Hunter to Hawaiian island natives, Young traveled the world over hunting for sharks.

Young got his first glimpse of a shark in 1885 when he was 10 years old. He became entranced with the creature then and remained intrigued for the next 77 years. To him, the shark was symbolic of all that he yearned for: the freedom, mystery, and exciting adventures that only the sea and its most ferocious predators could offer.

When Young was 16 years old, he developed a passion for catching sharks. He was working for the city of Honolulu then, hauling garbage out to sea in a barge and dumping the smelly load into waters infested with sharks. Scores of the hungry critters were always waiting at the same spot when feeding time arrived. Young used to watch them, fascinated at the monsters thrashing about and gorging themselves on the garbage. He caught them on handlines or harpooned them for sport. Later when word got around that he could capture big sharks with a harpoon, people became interested in the novelty and danger accompanying this kind of activity. Soon the sport developed and Young started operating scheduled charter trips, taking tourists out to sea and showing them how to harpoon man-eating sharks. This was long before the days of the sleek sportfishing cruisers whose anglers use rods and reels while trolling for oceanic game fish.

Young, enterprising by nature, was possessed with the idea of making a living from catching sharks. In addition to his charter operation, he removed their teeth, made all sorts of trinkets, and sold them to the tourists. The Chinese were always eager to buy the fins, the essential ingredient for their famous soups. Once he captured a large tiger shark, and after landing it the female gave birth to 42 pups. Young arranged to show the unusual exhibit at a fair in Waikiki and charged ten cents for admission. It was a success and he grossed $1,500 for the week that the fair lasted.

In 1920, Young finally discovered a way to make a full-time living hunting and catching sharks. After learning about the demand for sharkskin leather, he went to work for a firm in New Jersey that had recently developed a technique to process the skins. Manufacturers of leather goods saw a good future in using leather from the sea to meet popular fashion demands. Because of his experience with sharks, the firm sent him all over the world to locate the most heavily populated shark areas and establish commercial shark-fishing stations. Young's ambition was realized as he learned and taught assembly-line techniques for catching sharks.

He spent a good part of his life traveling and learning more about the peculiarities of sharks. Nobody in the world knew more about them than Young. He recorded his many observations and contributed a great deal of valuable knowledge to science. Later he wrote of his thrilling adventures and in 1933 his book *Shark! Shark! (The. Thirty Year Odyssey of a Shark Hunter)* was published. The book was bound in sharkskin and is now a collector's item. It was the only authentic treatment of a subject which was, at that time, based mostly on myth and legend. Young's personal knowledge and experiences paved the way for others to conduct research and develop effective commercial fishing methods.

When Young went into retirement, he still remained active in his work with sharks. At the age of 70, he continued his lectures and held audiences spellbound with his many exciting experiences. When World War II broke out, he assisted the U.S. Navy with their important research on repellents, a vital part of survival equipment. He also served as a consultant to the many firms who were catching sharks for the vitamin A in their livers.

In 60 years, Captain Young caught over 100,000 sharks and, at one time, was considered to be the world's foremost authority on them. When he passed away at the age of 87, he was cooperating with other well-known writers on another book of major significance.

Kane Mano accomplished what few men ever achieve. His avocation and vocation meshed in such a way that he was able to spend his whole life doing what he enjoyed most—hunting sharks.

Every time the subject of slaying sharks single-handedly is discussed, someone invariably raises a question of long standing: Can a man underwater, armed with only a knife, kill or seriously injure a sizable shark? A dispute often follows as skeptics jeer at the idea and some experts state that the feat is nearly impossible. The reasoning behind these opinions stems from the premise that "a shark's skin is too tough for a knife to penetrate." In addition, they say, the water offers too much resistance to the swift movement that is required to make a forceful thrust.

Actually, under the right conditions, there is no reason why a sharp knife in the hands of a strong man underwater cannot kill or seriously injure an attacking shark. Even women have been known to accomplish the feat and, possibly, have saved their lives by doing so! There are many stories about the famous Japanese female pearl divers who—for generations—have protected themselves against sharks with sharp knives as their only weapons.

However, accomplishing this deed successfully underwater requires split-second timing and the generation of enough force by either the man or shark to penetrate the tough skin. In other words, if a shark rushes by and a sharp knife is firmly implanted in it at the right angle, the shark's own momentum is sufficient to create a deep, long gash large enough to spill out its own entrails.

Single-handed shark disembowelment is not a new idea. South Sea natives have been doing it for centuries not only to save their own skins but in conjunction with ancient religious and ceremonial rites. During World War II, there were numerous instances of men ripping open shark bellies to defend themselves. The French Underground frogmen often encountered man-eating sharks in the warm waters of the Mediterranean Sea while attaching explosives to the hulls of enemy vessels. And there are several U.S. Navy frogmen and Underwater Demolition Team specialists who claim to have killed sharks with a knife in the South Pacific area.

It was only recently that an exciting account of shark disembowelment by man appeared in the newspapers. The story had such an ironic twist that it made headlines all over the world.

John Fairfax, Britain's famous oarsman (who rowed across the Atlantic by himself), is a professional adventurer and a fearless one as his most recent escapade proved. He has joined the ranks of that exclusive group of people who have killed sharks single-handedly using only a knife.

During his famous Atlantic crossing, Fairfax realized that his progress was being slowed by the continual growth of barnacles on the bottom of his boat. So, occasionally, he jumped overboard to scrape them off with his knife. It was on one of these occasions that he saw a fairly large shark coming toward him. He had brought his knife up to hit it on the nose when, suddenly the shark swerved. As Fairfax continued to stiff-arm his knife, the shark accidentally impaled itself upon the blade ripping its belly open and laying bare its vitals by the force of its own momentum. The shark sank slowly from sight and died. When he was interviewed by reporters, Fairfax admitted freely that the manner in which he had killed the shark was accidental.

The newspapers headlined the story and then quoted several unname experts and skeptics who declared that the feat was either improbable or downright impossible. This ruffled Fairfax's feathers and he announced that he would re-enact the dramatic incident if the newspapers would come up with a $25,000 stake. He was willing to endanger his life and prove that he could kill another shark if sufficient inducement was offered. Under prearranged conditions he felt that he as the aggressor would have an advantage over the shark because the element of surprise was in his favor.

The newspapers declined to accept his challenge. Fairfax was furious and began a personal vendetta against the newspapers. He was quoted as saying, "I don't know if I'll be able to kill the shark but, if I can, I'll bloody well drop its body at the newspaper's door. I'm a professional adventurer and it matters to me if something important I say isn't believed. They're accusing me of being a bloody liar. I can only prove I'm not by trying to do it again."

Months later, he made good his claim. And the newspapers and their quoted skeptics ate crow! With photos, movies, and witnesses in tow, Fairfax dumped a ripe eight-foot disemboweled hammerhead shark on the front lawn of one of the newspaper offices. He had killed the hammerhead in the Bahama Islands by encouraging it to attack him while he attracted it with a bloody grouper.

Fairfax is only one of a number of people who have put their lives on the line and destroyed a shark single-handedly. There are some people (courageous or foolish—I'm not sure which) in this world who will tackle a killer shark single-handedly if enough money is involved.

François Poli, the French writer and shark fisherman who wrote *Les Requins Se Pêchent La Nuit* (Sharks Are Caught at Night) relates a vivid, remarkable incident that he witnessed in a remote coastal fishing village in Haiti.

He tells of one of the villagers, a large Negro fisherman called

Sambo, who claimed that he had killed a total of 30 sharks while armed only with a double-bladed knife ten inches long.

When Sambo could find enough tourists or local citizens to raise $100, he would put on an exhibition for them by killing a large, hungry shark before their eyes.

A few days were required for the unusual preparations. With the help of some of the villagers, Sambo started feeding the sharks that usually cruised about an inlet near a channel leading to a shallow lagoon. He threw chunks of rotten meat to the sharks to encourage them to swim up into the channel. Eventually he would coax one to enter the small lagoon and trap it there by blocking off the outlet with several large wooden planks.

Sambo always explained that a few more days of waiting were necessary for the shark to become acclimated to his new surroundings and for it to develop a voracious appetite. He added that if his act was to be a success, the shark must be hungry and aggressive enough to attack him.

Although Sambo bore a few terrible scars from previous *corridas*, he had learned from experience how to sidestep his attacker so that now he was quite agile and proficient in his unusual occupation.

Finally the day of the big event arrived and Sambo formally announced to the villagers that the "moment of truth" was near! The villagers and tourists who had paid their fees assembled at the lagoon to watch Sambo play his game with death.

The crowd watched as the big shark cruised nervously about the lagoon in search of food. Its sinister dorsal fin sliced through the water and the spectators who lined the banks drew back a few steps whenever the man-eater swerved toward them.

Slowly and calmly Sambo entered the waist-deep lagoon and stopped, his knife poised dramatically, as he waited for the shark to find him. The audience was silent as the grim performance was about to begin, although some moved their lips in prayer and the sign of the cross was made many times. Sambo crouched low and shuffled his feet on the bottom to attract the shark's attention. The beast picked up the vibrations and zeroed in on Sambo. As the shark swirled to make a grab at Sambo's thigh, Sambo sidestepped quickly, brought his knife forward and plunged it deep into the shark's throat. The shark's momentum impaled it on the knife and, as the forward movement continued, its belly was ripped wide open along its entire length!

The timing was perfect and Sambo was untouched. He scrambled up the embankment to collect his fee from an audience still transfixed at the sight of the floundering monster writhing and twisting among its own entrails in the blood-stained water.

Poli went on to state that exhibitions of this kind are relatively common in many parts of the world and that the hand-to-hand struggle between man and shark is an old Polynesian custom revived in the twentieth century.

7
Sharks on a Tight Line

BEFORE THE DAWN OF CIVILIZATION, SOMEWHERE ALONG THE TIGRIS-Euphrates River, man's primitive instincts lusted for the hunt and the kill. Although other fish were plentiful, the robust shore-dweller also caught big sharks for sport and for food. He fashioned crude hooks of heavy animal bone and strong lines from vines of the trees. If he was too lazy to use his dugout canoe to get his bait out into deeper water, he rigged a crude kite made from tree leaves and flew his baited hook out over the waters, maneuvering it into the desired position.

Ancient man was an ingenious guy who loved to hunt and fish, especially when dangerous predators lurked in the waters at his doorstep. Like a contestant in our present day "Jaycee" shark tournaments, he, too, probably fished for sharks to help reduce the hazards of attacks on his fellow tribesmen. To speculate further, the tribe may have kept accounts of shark attacks similar to our present-day records. Since there were no tourists who might react in horror to sharks being caught in quantity, open war was waged continually against the critters. This may have been the origin of sportfishing for sharks. Today, in many areas along our coastline, local community ordinances oppose the idea of shark-fishing, and offer no incentive to the angler who would like to tangle with one of the monsters. These communities are afraid that the publicity of shark-fishing will drive the tourists away.

But regardless of the objections of prudent resort merchants who cater to the sun-and-surf crowd, the shark is emerging dramatically from the shadows. Apparently, he's becoming something of an international celebrity, even appearing on the postage stamps of many foreign countries. Usually cast as a crafty and diabolical villain, he has his good points: contributing valuable information for medical research, providing an exciting sport for the angler and, in many countries, serving as an important food source.

With the rapid distribution of present-day news media, shark news

151

travels swiftly. It is always exciting reading, since the shark is a choice subject for some reporters to twist into stories filled with sensationalism and ballyhoo. For centuries, the word *shark* has struck a chill in the hearts of many people. One might say that the feeling is akin to the fear of a lion or tiger. Modern man, like his ancient ancestors, enjoys the challenge of hunting these man-eaters either in the jungle with a gun or on the ocean using rod and reel. Since the rod-and-reel method requires considerable amounts of guts, muscle, and coordination, this activity can be classified as a genuine sport.

In our vast fishing fraternity there are thousands of anglers who are devoted to the growing sport of shark-fishing. "Sharkers" consider many of the species as genuine game, and fishing for them in a class by itself. In their minds they are not angling for just another fish but for a wild and unpredictable creature. They are correct for, biologically speaking, a shark is not a true bony fish but a hostile and carni-

Some countries feature sharks on their postage stamps. This species, the Lake Nicaragua shark, is one of the few that became fully adapted to living in fresh water. Ironically, it is credited with a long list of fatal attacks upon people.

In England, the sport of shark-fishing began here at Looe, Cornwall, where the Shark Angling Club of Great Britain has its official headquarters. (Courtesy Shark Angling Club of Great Britain)

vorous marine animal, a weird throwback to prehistoric times. To a sharker, regular fishing is as tame as rabbit-hunting while sharking is like tangling with a Bengal tiger!

Shark-fishing is gaining rapidly in popularity throughout the world. Every day anglers are joining the growing ranks of sharkers. There are dozens of organized shark-fishing clubs in the United States, and anglers in such countries as Great Britain, Australia, New Zealand, The Republic of South Africa, and Mexico are banding together and joining in the fun and adventure. These anglers are continually hanging up respectable rod-and-reel records. Even anglers in some of the remote countries of South America are enjoying this exciting sport. If an international shark-fishing association could be organized to weld these enthusiastic groups together, some excellent objectives could be attained: better public relations on an international basis, improved conservation, and a valuable food source for the undernourished peoples of the world. Most of the critters are edible and high in nutritional value and could therefore be an important food once the original reluctance is overcome. At the same time, marine scientists would have an inexhaustible supply of specimens for their important research studies.

Shark-fishing is quite popular along the coast of The Republic of

South Africa, most of the action taking place in the harbor of Durban, a well-known whaling port. Over the years, countless whaling ships have towed huge carcasses into port—followed by hordes of sharks that have vectored in on the blood traces left in the wakes of the vessels. The area is an obvious favorite for sharks because they can mutilate the dead whales or wait patiently for an easy handout.

Jutting out 2,000 feet from the beach at Durban is the famous South Pier, a concrete block breakwater 40 feet wide. Many anglers have made shark-fishing history from this celebrated spot. A large number of white sharks (called "blue pointers" by the local citizens) in excess of 500 pounds have been caught here and occasionally a thousand-pounder is captured. At the present time the pier record is a 1,660-pound white. Although other shark species are abundant in the harbor (such as the notorious Zambezi shark responsible for most of the attacks upon swimmers and the sand tigers, black-tipped, and hammerheads), the white is the "reel" target of the Durban sharker.

Whale meat is the popular bait used for whites, but not because it is easy to obtain. Local sharkers know that white sharks prefer the flesh of mammals (whale, blackfish, porpoise, or seal) over fish.

Some Durban anglers when fishing for sharks use extra-long rods measuring up to 15 feet. This provides them with much more leverage than conventional types. By using a longer rod, they can wrap one leg around the long butt, sit on it and, with a rocking motion, pump their quarry in with greater efficiency and less strain.

Until about ten years ago, Swedish anglers were enjoying shark-fishing in their local waters. Today they have to leave the country if they want to pursue this sport successfully. In those days, the porbeagle shark provided top rod-and-reel action as it was almost the biggest game fish around except for the sleepy Greenland and basking sharks. Unfortunately, the porbeagle population diminished quickly under the heavy pressure of commercial interests engaged in longline methods. Without a strong conservation program, the species nearly became extinct. Even the commercial interests are forced to fish in distant waters if they want to make a reasonable catch.

Olof Johansson, one of Sweden's leading angler-journalists informed me that, despite the rapid depletion of game sharks in their waters, there is still a strong and growing interest in shark-fishing among the anglers of his country. Many Swedish anglers who are serious about shark-fishing take their fishing holidays expressly for the pursuit of sharks. Some travel as far as Portugal, England, or even Ireland to fish. He also mentioned that the Canary Islands have recently become a hot spot for sharkers. These islands are popular because of the huge infestation of blues and hammerheads.

Shark-fishing is relatively new in Ireland and it is only in the last few years that the sport has achieved popularity in that country. Now,

Cecil Jacobs, charter member of the renowned Durban Shark Angling Club, was the first to land a 1,000-pound shark in South Africa. Using only 81-pound test line, Jacobs whipped the great white from Durban's South Pier. (Photo by Reg Harrison)

anglers from nearby countries on the continent who are no longer able to find any decent fishing in their own waters flock to the coast of Ireland to wet their lines and participate in the intriguing sport that offers a wide variety of species.

Ireland is keenly aware of the important potential that exists in shark-fishing and has undertaken certain conservation measures to perpetuate the sport. Studies are being made of the distribution, eating habits, and characteristics of the existing shark population and extensive tagging programs have been initiated to determine their migratory patterns.

So, Ireland is coming on strong in the "sharks for sport" scene. I've had some highly informative correspondence with Mr. Des Brennan, organizing controller of the Ireland Fisheries Trust, Inc. He informs me that the blue shark (*Prionace glauca*) is the main attraction for shark aglers. The real action begins in June and continues through September. Most of the blue sharks are caught in deep water and some are fairly respectable in size.

The tope (*Galeorhinus galeus*) is also a popular shark caught in most waters surrounding the country. Tope is a species very similar to both the soupfin shark (*Galeorhinus zyopterus*), found from the lower coast of Alaska to central California, and to the Australian school shark (*Galeorhinus australis*). Irish and foreign anglers find the tope exceptionally good sport since it offers a good scrap and is found in

A hefty blue shark is boated off Kinsale, Co. Cork. (Courtesy Irish Tourist Board)

moderate abundance. It is taken mostly from boats, but in many places can be caught by shore anglers from beaches, rock jetties, and in the estuaries. The best fishing for tope begins in late May and continues to October, with a stray one caught now and then during the winter months.

Although porbeagle sharks (*Lamna nasus*) are prolific in Irish waters, they manage to elude the anglers. Fishing for them is still in the experimental stages. They are being studied by the Ireland Fisheries Trust, which is investigating the angling potential of this species that offers such excellent sport. Porbeagles are caught in the Irish Sea and are found almost anywhere along the Irish coast, but only a few are caught by anglers.

Even makos (*Isurus oxyrinchus*) and threshers (*Alopias vulpinus*) have been encountered in Irish waters, but seldom landed. Despite the lack of information and shark-fishing techniques for these particular game species, prospects appear exceptionally good for anglers as long as there is a generous population and the challenge to catch them continues.

Although the mako is not the largest of the clan, he is probably one of the most sought-after sharks in the sea. A pelagic species, he may roam about the ocean for thousands of miles, making him a rare and elusive critter. In tribute to his strength and stamina, he is often called a "sea-going engine"! For spectacular leaps and swift enduring runs, the mako can't be beat. Some big-game anglers who are devoted to fishing for the great blue-fin tuna will pause in their pursuit, change their strategy and chase after a mako if one is sighted in the area. The mako is definitely in the same class of great game fishes as the broadbill swordfish, marlin, sailfish, and tarpon. Some anglers even rate the mako higher.

New Zealand anglers are entitled to boast about their proliferating mako shark population and about the tremendous size that this species attains. Even Zane Grey, famous writer of deep-sea fishing adventures and Western novels, eulogized the splendid catches he made in New Zealand waters—which, at the time, were considered angling feats worthy of record.

Makos are found in almost all the warm waters of the world but, if official record catches are any indication, the really big ones are "down under" along the coast of New Zealand.

A 1,000-pound mako caught by Doug Ross in 1943 held the I.G.F.A. All-Tackle World Record for 27 years. Only recently, his record was eclipsed by a mako that went 1,061 pounds, caught by James Penwarden. Another large mako taken off New Zealand weighed 820 pounds and was caught by T. Culshaw in 1964, also an I.G.F.A. World Record on 80-pound test line.

Doug Ross of New Zealand with his 1,000-pound mako shark. This I.G.F.A.
all-tackle world record stood unbroken for 27 years! (Courtesy D. Ross)

In over 20 years of fishing on the saltwater scene, my customers and
I have caught only a few dozen makos of mentionable size. Although
most of them were caught in Pacific waters, all the larger ones were
taken on the Atlantic Coast. In most cases the makos were caught by

conventional trolling methods while searching for other game fish. When we did bump into one it was unintentional, but most of my anglers were quite determined to land it. Then, after they had once sampled the game qualities of the critter, they always insisted that we fish again expressly for mako. Many were so delighted that they had their catches mounted and hung next to cherished marlins or sailfish.

Aside from the fact that it probably offers considerably more resistance to being captured than most other game fish, the scarcity of the mako is another reason why an angler will want it mounted. This qualifies it as a prize trophy for any den.

Most game sharks are rather handsome-looking creatures, in a frightening sort of way; perfectly streamlined and powerfully built. Even when mounted with mouths open (baring many fierce teeth) and with cold, glassy eyes staring blankly ahead, they seem to give the impression that they are still fighting to live and defying capture.

Fish taxidermy is as old as the first happy angler who wanted to display his prize. Only in recent years, however, has the industry become a highly specialized field. Fish are no longer "stuffed." With the inception of moulding processes, new plastic resins and color preservatives, fish taxidermy has improved tremendously. Since the process is now a complicated and exacting art, each specimen is handled scrupulously with the fine tools and skills of the craftsman employed to fashion a complete and true-to-life product of lasting beauty. Practically all coloration in a fish disappears after death, so a good taxidermist must be able to duplicate the intricate and delicate coloring that nature originally infused into her creatures. A skilled taxidermist will even give the mount the personality peculiar to that particular species. Only a well-established and experiencd man should be consulted for a mount preparation. Considering the time and effort expended by the taxidermist, the expense is well worth it!

The remora is an unusual creature but it is not a parasite. It is simply a species of sea "hitch-hiker" with a suction apparatus on the top of its head. Although frequently called a "shark Remora," its choice of hosts is not confined to sharks. It is often found on other sea creatures such as the billfishes, dolphins, mackerels, rays, and even the slow, lumbering turtles.

The remora must be an excellent swimmer since it is capable of attaining the speeds of the swift pelagic billfishes and dolphins in order to "hitch a ride." After a fish or shark has been landed, one or two remoras are often found clinging tenaciously to their late host. Probably nature, in one of her many strange ways, created the suction adapter because the remora is unable to travel long distances alone. Therefore, we have a creature that can attain great speeds for a short period of time, but one that may lack endurance.

A mounted shark head makes an impressive display as well as an interesting conversation piece. Taxidermists usually form the end on an angle, giving the impression that the shark is emerging obliquely from the wall. The above specimen is a good example of a bull shark.

In the remora-shark relationship, as with some of the other fish, the remora is the active member and the shark is the passive one. This is known as *commensalism*. It means that two creatures share the same environment and food in a nonparasitic relationship but only one creature really benefits. In this case, the remora depends upon the shark (and/or other large fish) for locomotion and, usually, for its food. As the shark begins feeding, the remora flexes its louverlike plates, releases its hold on its host and scrounges on the scraps that are left.

The remora's suction-disk apparatus is a remarkable mechanism. Some of our present-day engineering designs are based on the principle of its mechanical action. Its suction power is so strong that some of the West Indian natives are able to capture turtles by securing a line to a remora and allowing it to attach itself to a free-swimming turtle!

Those of us who spend a lot of time on the water see billfishes, rays, and sharks thrashing about, trying to shake off the remoras clinging to them. Evidently the remoras must cause some annoyance to their

A good example of nature's engineering talents is the remora's suction-disc apparatus. This remarkable mechanism has inspired some of the mechanical principles found in today's technology.

hosts. The black-tipped spinners (which exhibit this particular reaction more than other sharks) have the unique ability to jump completely clear of the water and to spin in midair in an attempt to free themselves of their hitch-hiking companions.

Remoras are rarely seen unless they are attached to their hosts, although they are caught frequently by anglers who specialize in bottom fishing. Occasionally, remoras can be spotted in the drifting chum when it is spilled into the water. Once in the chum line, they lose their timidity and will take a piece of cut bait eagerly. At times they even approach the chum bag and nip at the small particles as they emerge.

Wise anglers, who see one or more remoras swimming in their fishing area, know that a larger fish or shark is hovering about in the vicinity. Quickly, they prepare adequate bait and try to capture the suspected "host," lurking near by.

The endurance and strength of a shark have always been controversial subjects among anglers. Questions often arise: How hard does a shark actually pull? or How much exertion, measured in pounds, does a shark really apply? Some writers, praising the "fight" of a shark, exaggerate when they try to describe the antics of a thrashing shark on the end of a line. You can read descriptions such as: "Boats have been towed for miles;" "Anglers have been yanked into the sea, barely escaping with their lives;" "Docks have been ripped apart losing 30 feet of heavy timber;" "One-inch manilla rope was snapped like a thread;" etc. I don't doubt that some of these remarkable incidents actually took place but I just don't believe that they took place as often or under some of the circumstances as claimed.

In his book, *Tigers of the Sea*, Colonel Hugh Wise wrote of his experiments with several sharks. He conducted many extensive tests using spring scales to measure the actual pull that a shark exerts when hooked and struggling for its freedom. For utmost accuracy, he made these measurements in fractions of a pound. Although the readings on the scale often fluctuated from high to low as the shark tired, Wise did get some average figures.

He used sand sharks that weighed about 250 pounds. The initial pull measured as much as 150 pounds, but with constant resistance upon the line, the tension dropped quickly and stayed about 50 pounds.

Basing his calculations upon these figures, Wise speculated that a shark weighing twice as much as the 250 pound specimen used in the experiment would average twice the pulling force. This would be about 100 pounds for the larger creature. He also used his experiments to arrive at a "pound-for-pound" figure. The maximum force was approximately one-half pound pull per pound of shark weight, or an average of one-third pound pull per pound. These results demonstrate a fair amount of power even though a sand shark probably doesn't put up the same fight and resistance that other species have been known to exhibit.

Later, Colonel Wise made an interesting experiment when he tested the acrobatic swordfish, which ranks as one of the world's leading game fish and compared it with the shark's strength. His summation indicated that sharks are more difficult to conquer than leaping swordfish. The swordfish exhausts himself by jumping while the shark's energy is conserved by intermittent resting periods.

Other experiments by Stewart Springer, a well-known shark expert, demonstrated the impressive strength of sharks. He used a device called a dynamometer to measure the pull and discovered that a 10-foot hammerhead could exert a pull of 1,500 pounds and that a 350-pound silky shark could snap a rope testing approximately 1,350 pounds!

In conclusion, when considering pound-for-pound exertion upon a line, there are few fish (possibly none) that can equal the strength and endurance of the shark. Therefore, it is easy to see why some anglers do not enjoy the long struggle offered by the stubborn resistance of a shark. They prefer to fish for game that offers less resistance to capture and they avoid anything involving "dead weight" or "too much work"!

The name Mundus is renowned among the many devoted shark anglers in America. Nicknamed the Monster Man of Montauk, Captain Frank Mundus of Montauk, New York, has contributed more to the grawing popularity of shark-fishing as a sport than anyone I know. He has put the I.G.F.A. crown on the heads of dozens of anglers who, because of his expert instruction, captured huge sharks on light tackle from his charter boat, *Cricket II*.

Mundus not only introduced sportfishing for sharks to the fishing fraternity, but pioneered the use of light tackle to subdue the brutes. After years of praising the game qualities of many species, he was among those instrumental in getting the I.G.F.A. to recognize some of the present species as game fish.

Since introducing thousands of anglers (now confirmed sharkers) to the sport, Mundus has become one of the most popular shark-fishing skipper-guides in the world. He has been mentioned countless times in periodicals and books, while many of his adventures with anglers and sharks have been published in their entirety. Mundus and his customers have caught over 20,000 blue sharks during the last 20 years. This figure does not include the many hammerheads, makos, browns, duskies, porbeagles, and whites that were also caught on his "shark safaris." No count was made on the latter species, but the number must be staggering.

One day Mundus steamed proudly into port with a giant white shark lashed to the side of his sturdy boat. This was probably the biggest living thing ever brought into Montauk Point. Unable to find anyone who would "tackle" the monster, Mundus and his mate had harpooned it and spent many difficult hours in making the extraordinary capture. The white weighed 4,500 pounds, measured 17½ feet in length, and had a girth of 13 feet!

Dockside spectators were bug-eyed with awe at this man-eating goliath hanging from the hoist. The exciting news spread swiftly among anglers on Long Island and in New York State. Soon Mundus began receiving calls for reservations on the *Cricket*. Every sharker wanted a crack at breaking a world record. Mundus had proven, moreover, that big whites did exist in Long Island waters and that some were potential record-breakers!

Mundus always puts on a good show for his customers, especially if they have never seen his fishing strategy before. To lure a shark close to the boat, he often uses the entire carcass of a bluefin tuna. He ties a line to the tuna and lets it drift along behind he boat. When a

Captain Frank Mundus congratulates one of his happy customers for whipping a large white shark. Mundus, who operates his charterboat the Cricket II *from Montauk Point, New York, has brought in scores of white sharks exceeding 1,000 pounds. (Courtesy Lighthouse Photoshop)*

shark grabs for the tuna, Mundus tantalizes it by pulling on the line, creating a "tug-of-war." This commotion and frustration enrages the shark, usually attracts other sharks to the scene and provides exceptional action for his customers.

Mundus uses tons of chum every year. He prefers whale meat or blubber over any other kind of flesh to attract and bait sharks. Occasionally he harpoons a blackfish or a pilot whale, grinds it up with an electric grinder and stores the ground flesh in huge freezers. But if his customers wish to fish for records, he uses only trash fish or menhaden to chum up his sharks since I.G.F.A. rules prohibit the use of mammal flesh and blood.

Mundus began fishing at the tender age of 10 and has been at it ever since. During the past 20 years he has made shark-fishing a specialty, gained notoriety, and enhanced his reputation as a guide. If an angler wants to reserve his boat and take advantage of his expert advice, he should make his arrangements well in advance.

When I asked Mundus during one of his visits to the Florida Keys what motivated him to specialize in shark-fishing, he simply shrugged his shoulders and replied, "A lotta reasons, Hal. I guess mostly to make people happy. I enjoy seeing them catch something big, *really* big. Then there's the adventure and challenge, too. Shucks, you're doin' the same thing yourself. You oughta know why."

"You're right Frank," I agreed. "When we can put our anglers on to the biggest thing they've ever caught, our own egos are tickled!"

8

How To Catch Sharks for Sport

ALTHOUGH THE POPULARITY OF SPORTFISHING FOR SHARKS IS GROWING continually, there are still some anglers who look down their noses at the sport, not realizing how much fun and excitement sharking can be, Some anglers are downright belligerent in their attitude toward sharks; the proposal to catch them on sporting tackle infuriates them. Others stubbornly insist that angling for sharks is not a sporting proposition regardless of the kind of tackle employed. They refuse to participate in the activity as long as other game fish are available. All this dissension and repudiation of shark-fishing is caused by several, varied reasons, some of which are justified and even plausible.

A negative attitude can develop when an angler is unfamiliar with the different species of sharks and the proper tackle used in capturing them *safely* and skillfully. Some anglers, aware of the risks involved during a tussle, can't be bothered learning the proper methods of handling a shark to reduce the hazards of personal injury. Others are plain scared of the critters just as they are of a toothy five-pound barracuda that can also snap and draw blood! Yet this same angler eagerly tackles and whips a harmless 500-pound tuna if given the opportunity. He knows the worst that can happen to him is blisters on his hands (if he doesn't wear gloves) or a few cramped muscles! So a genuine fear of sharks exists among these timid anglers who cannot believe that sharking can be safe.

Another reason that some anglers won't recognize shark-fishing is because they still have vivid memories of the tactics used in the commercial shark-fishing industry over 20 years ago. The vision of the heavy cable lines, chains, ropes, and winches that were then necessary to catch big sharks productively distorted or destroyed any conception of how these monsters could be captured on regulation sporting gear. I agree that it is difficult for a prospective shark angler to disassociate himself from these images and change his perspective but, with a little tolerance on his part and persuasion on mine, we might meet on common ground.

So, in the following pages, I will make my pitch (successfully, I hope) and discuss in detail what I believe to be the necessary techniques involved in hunting, baiting, and landing dangerous sharks in a safe and sporting manner. I want to encourage the reader to accept the challenge of participating in this fascinating aspect of game-fishing.

Since we are dealing with a primitive creature of immense strength and stamina (much greater than many game fishes), whose powerful jaws and tail can cause not only havoc with equipment but serious injury to an angler (as found in any other related sport), the accent on safety will be emphasized continually throughout this chapter.

Like many other game fish, sharks migrate from one area to another in search of food, comfort, and for breeding purposes. Various species of sharks migrate at different times throughout the year just as fishes do. Therefore, a population of one or more species is usually present at any time in most areas of the tropical and temperate zones of the world.

The most practical method of locating sharks quickly is simply to make inquiries at the local fish-packing house. Commercial fishermen are always glad to cooperate with anyone who decides to reduce the shark population. Sharks continually frighten and chase schools of fish while the commercial fishermen are trying to set their nets. Fish become spooky and many manage to evade the surrounding nets. Sometimes sharks charge into a school of fish that have been trapped and, in the process of feeding, cause considerable damage to the nets. This can be extremely expensive for the fishermen. In many cases, the loss of fish and the damage to nets can put a business into bankruptcy.

Airplane pilots who operate sight-seeing trips along the coast are also good sources of information. Sharks are easily spotted from the air and a recent sighting can steer the angler to the action.

Almost all anglers and the personnel at bait-and-tackle shops are glad to point out where sharks have been seen or caught or where one just grabbed a trophy fish from some irate angler.

Most game species of sharks that inhabit inshore waters and flats are on the move continually in search of food and often come close to shore. They can be caught from jetties, shorelines, piers, bridges, or while wading the shallow flats. Fishing for sharks from these locations requires heavy tackle since the angler is in a fixed position where he has to practically "horse" his quarry in, which eliminates some of the sporting characteristics. But fishing for sharks from a boat is more practical and allows an angler to apply his skill using light tackle. His chances of landing a large shark are much better since he is able to maneuver his boat to make a capture easier.

Sharks can be caught from a boat by slow-trolling, drifting, or lying

Commercial fishermen, plagued continually by sharks that foul and tear their nets, would welcome commercial shark-fishing operations in their locales.

at anchor. Any method can be productive but, while trolling, the use of an attraction such as chum (ground-up oily fish) is impractical since a moving boat covers too much area to make the chum effective. When the boat is drifting or lying at anchor in a current, chumming is necessary to attract sharks to the baits.

There are a few species of sharks (such as the pelagic or open-ocean rovers) that can attain considerable speeds and these will grab at a fast-trolled bait. Other species are slower by nature and are seldom caught by fast-trolling methods. Almost all species will take a slow-trolled bait or a bait presented while drifting or lying at anchor so, for productive reasons, an angler will be exposed to more action while employing the latter procedures.

Since these restrict a boat's movements (and fishing is done almost from a standstill), sharks must be attracted to the immediate vicinity of the boat and encouraged to take one of the baited hooks. Herein lies the key to successful shark-fishing—the use of an effective attractant that will appeal to their well-developd sensory (lateris system) and olfactory (sense of smell) organs.

Nature has endowed the shark with keen sensorial equipment to assist it in locating food. This sonar-like mechanism enables it to detect low frequency sounds emitted by disabled fish. The sudden un-canny appearance of a shark upon the scene when a fish is hooked and struggling to free itself attests to the terrific efficiency of its receptive abilities. Therefore, a live struggling fish with a hook inserted under its dorsal fin makes an ideal bait for attracting any shark on the prowl. Some of the favorites are members of the jack and tuna families, yellow-tail snappers, grunts, ladyfish, and a host of other species that sharks love to devour.

The combination of a live bait struggling in a steady flow of chum drifting down current from the boat can attract a shark a mile away. This is especially true if the ground-up fish used for chumming pur-poses is oily in nature, such as menhaden (mossbunker) and mackerel and enriched with slaughterhouse blood. The oil creates a slick on the water that will travel in the current for miles before dissipating. The blood and small particles of ground fish carried away by the current slowly descend, eventually settling on the bottom. Chumming covers large areas of water both on the surface and at the bottom and is the most effective way to attract a shark's extremely sensitive sense of smell.

Chum can be bought at almost any coastal bait-and-tackle shop or commercial fish-packing house, which always provide their fishermen with chum to attract and encourage wary premium reef fish to bite. However, chum sold by the tackle shops or fish houses consists only of ground-up fish and contains very little blood. A shark angler, to increase his chances of attracting sharks, should "sweeten" his chum with blood.

Liquid, frozen, or dehydrated blood is sold at any slaughterhouse. Dehydrated blood can also be purchased from leading nurseries that use it to enrich their fertilizers and plant foods. Poultry ranches also sell blood which, when mixed with chicken entrails and fish chum, produces a tempting gruel that will drive any shark to licking his chops!

Although it is not available in many areas, chum made from ground-up whale and porpoise flesh is considered by most sharkers to be the best shark lure in the world. Sharks, having a natural penchant for these mammals, are known to follow them for hundreds of miles, patiently waiting for one to drop back from its school because of disability or injury. Shark anglers who wish to catch an official world-record shark, may *not* use the flesh or blood of a mammal for chumming purposes. The I.G.F.A. (International Game Fish Association) is quite adamant about this ruling.

The technique of chumming is almost an art in itself. Several factors and variables are involved that can increase or decrease the chances of attracting sharks to a baited hook. Changes in current velocities and wind which, in turn, can change the boat's rate of movement while drifting, must be observed continually while dispersing the chum. The oil slick must be maintained at all times while a steady flow of chum enters the water. Overchumming in a swift current can confuse sharks and delay them in locating the bait. A slow current requires more chum and oil (to reach the nose of a faraway shark) before most of it settles to the bottom. When no current exists or the tide changes, the boat must go on a wind drift in order to disperse the chum. While lying at anchor, if the tide changes and flows into or adjacent to the wind, then it becomes necessary to bridle the boat in such a position that the chum will flow astern and past the area where the baits are positioned. The ideal situation exists when the rate of chum dispersement is just enough to create a never-ending oil slick dead astern with a minimum amount of particles entering the water.

Some avid sharkers prepare and freeze their own chum. This is not only easy on the budget but is also a better mixture than they can buy commercially. They will save fish containing a high oil content, grind it up in a hand grinder, mix it with mammal blood, and freeze it for future use.

While waiting for a shark to strike, most anglers spend their time fishing for other game since the running chum also attracts fish. Many are caught in this way between shark catches. Pouring seawater over the fish lying in the box will add more essence to the chum as the blood and secretions from the fish will seep from the drain and spill out into the water. But the angler should never use a dead shark and its secretions to try to lure other sharks. After an hour in warm temperatures, a dead shark begins to decompose and exude ammonium acetate, which is capable of repelling other sharks.

Sharks are also attracted to sounds other than the vibrations emitted by injured fish or sea mammals. Some sharkers use waterproof fireworks such as cherry bombs or ash cans which, when lit, will explode under water and send sound vibrations considerable distances.

If no live bait is available, dead fish such as bonito, mackerel, jacks, ladyfish, and even catfish will catch hungry sharks whose appetites have been whetted by the strong flavors of the running chum. But this dead bait should be fresh, preferably unfrozen, to serve as a tasty morsel. Frozen bait will work but much of its flavor has been lost in the deep freeze.

Sometimes a shark will appear in the slick—"homing in" on one of the live baits. The frightened bait is fighting for its life and evading the shark at every pass. The shark may not be hungry enough to continue its attack and gives up the chase, a situation often encountered which dispels the theory that all sharks are voracious and will attack any crippled fish. As a result, live bait will not always prove effective in catching sharks, especially those that are sluggish by nature or those that may be curious but not particularly interested in feeding. A shark, like any other creature, can have a belly full of food and simply lose its appetite for more.

I've found that two bait presentations, one alive and one dead, placed out in the chum line have been the most effective method in

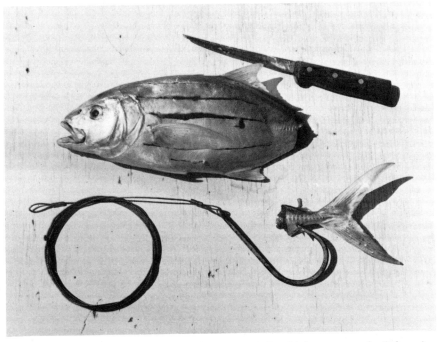

If a whole fish bait is used, the tail section should be removed. Otherwise, when a shark grabs the offering, the hook may tear the bait and become lodged in its hard tail section instead of becoming imbedded firmly in the shark's mouth. Dead bait should be slashed to release body juices, which enhance the attraction to sharks.

catching sharks, whether they are lazy and sluggish or voracious and hungry. Chances are, one type or the other will be caught using this double presentation.

Most experienced sharkers have a pretty good idea of what size shark they expect to encounter and will base the choice of their hook sizes upon this speculation. But, as a rule, because the mouth of a shark is so much larger than that of most game fishes, relatively larger hooks should be used. Sharks don't nibble on a bait, they simply engulf it (a rather gamey characteristic, I'd say) and seldom bypass the hook. They know what they want and proceed to inhale it without any scrutiny or ceremony.

Another basis for the use of large hooks stems from the great area of the mouth that is covered by teeth. If a hook isn't large enough, the many rows of teeth will deflect the point from the fleshy part of the mouth. A larger hook has a wider throat and will allow the point and barb to pass over the teeth and imbed elsewhere in the jaw, tongue, or throat. By the same token, the shank of the larger hook is more likely to be chewed, instead of the leader or cable secured to the eye of the hook. The leader often separates and the shark is lost.

Since a hook's sole function is to hook and hold the quarry, further consideration must be given to its specific size. The relation between the hook size and the tackle used is very important. The *length* of the barb of any hook (the holding part) is increased whenever a larger size is selected. This means that the rod and line must be strong enough to drive the barb "home" so that it will catch and hold. Therefore, a much smaller hook must be selected if lighter tackle is used. In other words, if balanced light tackle such as a 20-pound rod with 20-pound test line is used to whip a large shark, the hook must be smaller proportionately. Otherwise, the tackle won't be strong enough to seat the hook properly, resulting in a possible standoff. Conversely, if a heavy rod and line are used with a hook too small, the hook will catch properly but will bend, break, or simply pull out under the erratic pressures of a vigorous shark.

Hooks are never really sharp enough when taken from a new box, especially if they are to be used for shark-fishing. Therefore, hooks should be honed or filed needle sharp to effectuate deep penetration into the tough and gristly material that lines a shark's mouth.

Another recommendation to insure maximum hook penetration is to modify the round point by filing or grinding it to a triangular point. This creates three sharp cutting edges that will make penetration easier. Although some hook manufacturers make triangulated hooks, the points and edges still require some sharpening.

The eternal question remains: When do you strike and set the hook after a shark takes a bait? True, a shark seldom hesitates and often

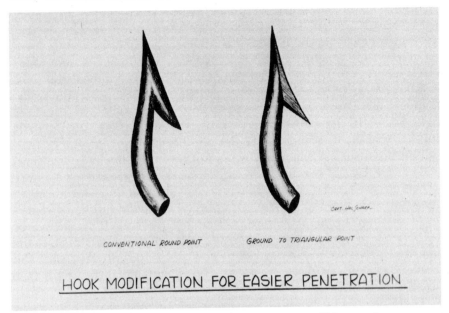

CONVENTIONAL ROUND POINT   *GROUND TO TRIANGULAR POINT*

HOOK MODIFICATION FOR EASIER PENETRATION

Triangulating hook barbs with a file or honing stone will insure deeper penetration in the tough jaws of a shark.

makes a wholesale grab at most baits whether they are alive or dead, but there are other factors involved such as: How much of a large bait does a small shark actually have in his mouth? or He has the bait—why doesn't he run with it? All species of sharks do not react in the same way when they take a bait. The timing also depends upon current conditions at the time. Naturally, if a shark takes a bait and runs up current with it toward the boat, a large amount of slack line is created. The hooks will never sink in if the line isn't retrieved swiftly until it becomes taut again. At this time the angler should execute his strike immediately in an effort to hook his shark before it runs under the boat or into the anchor line.

If the bait is large and the angler can see that a relatively small shark has made a grab for it, he must give the shark some time to suck it down. On the other hand, some of the sluggish species (the nurses, lemons, and bulls, large or small) will sometimes doodle around with a bait before inhaling it. Unfortunately, most of the time we cannot see what is actually taking place when a bait is struck, especially when the baits are presented in deep water. Sometimes a live bait will surface in an attempt to flee from its executioner. When the shark finally catches up with it, he usually engulfs if without further ado, and it is then that we know the hook should be set immediately.

Outside of these particular instances, there is really no definite set of rules as to when a shark should be struck. Much of it is pure guess-work, because all we know for sure are the conditions such as slack lines and velocity of currents. For this reason, excitement coupled with judgment only magnifies the challenge in trying to hook one of nature's oldest and strongest predators. One thing is certain, if the strike is fast (shown by the float tearing swiftly across the water or pulled under immediately) there is little to lose if the angler sets his hook right away. If the strike doesn't take, the shark will usually make another grab at it, giving the angler another chance.

This discussion of when and when not to set the hooks after a shark strikes at a bait also centers around a shark's individual personality. Different species of sharks exhibit different dispositions. One thing we know for sure, that all of them are unpredictable and can be extremely fickle in their behavior toward a dead or live bait. The old adage, "experience is the best teacher" holds true in this case. I'm not sure how much experience is needed to run up a 100-percent score. I've caught thousands of sharks and I'm still misjudging them—more than I care to admit!

There are several kinds of floats that can be used in shark-fishing to keep a bait suspended in the water. The float should be one that has an adjustable device so that it can be positioned anywhere on the line to regulate the depth of the bait. It should also be easy to remove to avoid entanglement during an engagement with a shark. But some-times an adequate float is difficult to find if large heavy baits are used. I don't believe there are any commercial floats made that will keep a five- or six-pound struggling jack from pulling it under.

Personally, I like to use regular five-cent balloons, which have many advantages while the expense is negligible. For one thing, when a shark runs off or sounds with the bait, the balloon pops and is out of the way. The chore of reaching out to remove a commercial float from the line is eliminated while maneuvering a shark alongside.

A balloon can be blown up to a size that will match the weight or vigorous movements of any size bait. It is elastic; therefore easy to tie and slide to any desired position on the line. It can also serve as a water kite, allowing the breeze to hold the balloon and a lively bait away from the boat.

Sometimes while we are lying bridled at anchor (to keep our stern as close as possible toward the running current) the tidal current will be running in the opposite direction to the wind. This situation always creates a kind of standoff for keeping a bait from moving too close to the boat. Depending upon the briskness of the wind, I may employ as many as three or four balloons, using the wind as an advantage to counteract the current, and keep my baits in the desired position in the chum slick.

There are two obvious reasons why metal leaders are a necessary part of shark-fishing tackle. The sharp cutting edges of a shark's teeth will sever any soft leader. (Occasionally their teeth will even cut through a wire leader.) And wire will resist abrasions caused by the rough denticles of a shark's hide.

Short lengths of wire leader are fine when fishing for small sharks using light tackle such as spinning gear or a flyrod. But for the larger sharks, 100 pounds and up, stainless-steel braided wire or cable leader is recommended not only for its strength but because it is practically kink proof. The jumping and acrobatic gyrations of the mako or spinner shark can kink a wire leader regardless of its gauge or strength and result in the loss of the gamester.

Cable leaders come in various gauges and strength tests and are made up of several strands of wire. These leaders can be purchased in packaged kits containing the recommended sleeves for crimping the ends when making a loop or for attachment to a hook. The leaders test from 75 pounds up to 250 pounds; the latter is able to hold any reasonably sized shark. However, as cable leaders go, even the 250-pound test is still considered lightweight material. If one or more strands of the braided wire is severed by a shark's teeth, the leader is weakened considerably and can break at a crucial moment. A frayed cable leader with one or more severed strands usually won't break under the pressure caused by a fighting shark, but when a crew member grabs the leader to "horse" the shark within gaffing range, the extra pressure on the leader causes it to break.

Another disadvantage exists when using braided wire or lightweight cable leaders. When one or more of the wire strands breaks, small sharp ends appear and can play havoc with the hands while handling the leader whether gloves are worn or not.

To avoid breakage and cut hands, I use a much heavier cable whose strands are proportionately larger in diameter and less likely to break or to be severed by shark's teeth. This cable is usually manufactured for the aircraft industry and contains a rich chrome content that makes it a high-grade, stainless-steel wire. It can be purchased in bulk form on spools of various lengths and strength tests. When I anticipate catching sharks of 200 pounds or more, I use 600-pound test aircraft cable exclusively. The material is expensive but the cost is justified in the reduction of breakage and the chance of cutting the hands. This material and matching sleeves can be purchased at any large marine supply house and proper crimping pliers can be found in hardware stores.

For general shark-fishing purposes, a cable leader should measure at least 15 feet in length. If longer sharks are suspected in the area, then it is advisable to use longer leaders. This serves as protection against the abrasive hide of a shark if it should rub or become tangled by the shark's erratic movements. A long leader is also advantageous

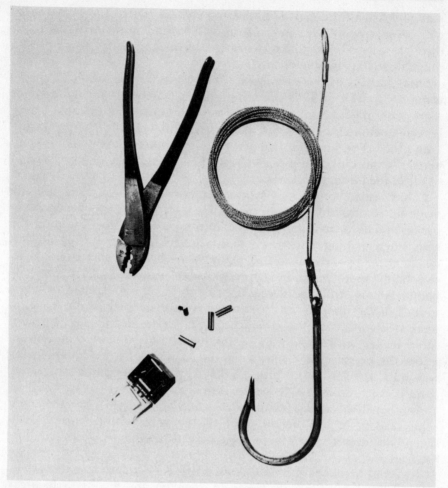

The proper use of crimping pliers and matching sleeves is important in making slip-proof cable leaders for shark-fishing.

during the landing operation when the crew manhandles a shark alongside for gaffing or dispatchment. A double line of 12 to 15 feet also assists the handling of a large shark and serves as added protection against breakage when the critter wraps up in the leader or tail slaps the line.

The I.G.F.A. angling rules pertaining to leaders, are more than generous as shown by the following rule number 4:

"The leader and the double line on all weights of tackle up to and including the 50-pound line test class, shall be limited to 15 feet of double line and 15 feet of leader. For heavier tackle, the line shall not be doubled at the leader end for more than 30 feet and the leader shall not exceed 30 feet".

Because of the possibility of injury to whoever is handling the leader while bringing a shark alongside for gaffing or dispatching, I'm going to inject a word of caution at this point. Time and again throughout this book I've emphasized how rugged, strong, and unpredictable sharks can be. Because of their strength, they can yank a crew member from the cockpit into the water. What would ensue is anyone's guess.

In the first place, gloves should be used at all times for protection against leader cuts and burns. When the double line comes within reach it should be grasped firmly and brought in hand over hand slowly and evenly. *At no time should the double line or leader be wrapped around one of the hands for a better grip.* If this occurs and if a well-hooked violent shark suddenly makes a run, there is no holding him and someone is going to be minus a hand or fingers or wind up in the water with a very enraged shark.

If the shark wants to run and it appears that he is poorly hooked, then the line or leader should be dropped immediately to allow the angler to play his quarry and bring it back within reach of the double line for another attempt at gaffing. This should be done as many times as necessary to be certain that the shark won't throw the hook while the double line or leader is in the hands of the crew member. In this way the loss of a shark alongside puts the responsibility upon the angler. Naturally, if it is seen that the shark is well hooked, then it can be hand-lined smartly for gaffing or dispatchment.

A good boatman must always cooperate with the mate or crew member and work as a team in boating a shark or any other game fish. The boat must be maneuvered in such a way as to give the angler and mate every possible advantage in whipping a shark. The quarry must be fought off the stern within two or three points on either side to keep the shark from going under the boat or becoming tangled in the underwater machinery.

As soon as the mate has the double line or leader in his hands, the angler should adjust his drag mechanism immediately to reduce the tension on the reel spool, which reduces the pressure on the shark. This practice will help prevent the hook from pulling out (especially if it's only lip-hooked) if the mate is forced to release his hold when the shark makes a sudden lunge. In other words, if the tension of the drag isn't reduced, the inertia caused by a "dead" reel spool whose drag remained tight will create a sudden shock upon the hook when the shark exerts any movements, forcing the reel spool to turn again. The inertia of the reel alone could be enough for the hook to pull out and the shark will be lost.

When an angler sets out to lick a big shark, much more is involved than pitting strength against strength. Coordination, familiarity with equipment, and a knowledge of some of the basic laws of physics play vital roles. Knowing when to apply the line pressure on a shark, how long to keep it up, and when to relax the pressure as the tension approaches the breaking point are essential elements in the technique of breaking its spirit.

The pressure is controlled by proper drag settings on the reel. In addition, the extra drag created by the bending rod plus the added resistance of the water upon the line must be taken into account when making drag adjustments. These are fine points to consider when whipping a heavy shark or any large fish. The whole endeavor involves a lot of wear and tear on muscles and tempers, but proper technique *must* be employed if record catches are to be made.

The angler must realize that the reel is simply a device that stores the line, geared with a high ratio and a drag assembly consisting of friction clutch plates that will create an increased tension while the line is running out. Actually the reel has nothing to do with bringing in the game. It becomes functional only when the game is pulling upon the drag setting. The experienced angler adjusts his drag mechanism constantly in addition to applying pressure on the line with his gloved hand, while tied into a fish and knows approximately how much resistance is required in the drag while measuring the pressure induced by these factors: the game at the end of his line; water resistance upon the line; and the added resistance created by the bending rod. It should be mentioned that all these are variables and require some quick estimations in order for the angler to cope with them successfully.

There is still another factor to consider while making drag adjustments. If it is ignored it may blow the angler's chance of breaking the shark's spirit. Anyone familiar with basic physics or the simple law of pulleys knows that the tension upon the reel spool and drag steadily increases as line is running out and the diameter of the spool becomes smaller. Exactly how much tension in pounds pull is created only a mathematician could solve, but this can be a critical factor. The angler can expect his line to break if he doesn't use good judgment in making the correct adjustments while his shark is running off with 200 or 300 yards of line before he can put a dent into its spirit!

Aside from muscle, the rod does the work of bringing in the game. Coordination and timing, while pumping the rod to pick up the slack line, are the keys to expert handling of the tackle. Knowing when to pull up on the rod or when to drop it depends completely upon the angler's ability to feel the shark's head creating the resistance. He must know just how much pressure can be applied to begin the long, drawn-out process of breaking the shark's spirit before popping the line. The experienced angler will study the breaking limits of his rod and line by observing the arc or bend while someone pulls upon the line with a scale to measure the maximum tension just before the breaking point. Familiarity with equipment cannot be overemphasized, especially when going after record sharks on light tackle.

To measure how much his line can take from a given drag setting before breakage occurs, an angler can "dry run" his reel and rod with a scale test and come up with some pretty accurate figures. He can determine the breaking point of his line on a particular drag setting in pounds at any given spool diameter by simply using a tension scale secured to the line running off the rod tip. The wise angler goes through these preliminary motions so that he can become better acquainted with the operation and dependability of his equipment.

The technique of landing a large shark can be accomplished safely and simply. I find that, after a shark is brought alongside the boat, a regular shark gun is the safest and most efficient method to dispatch it. This may raise an eyebrow or two in some quarters of the angling fraternity (unjustly, I believe), but in dealing with dangerous creatures such as these I feel sincerely that the safest measures should be employed in the landing of a large shark. In most big-game fish tournaments, when the mate has his hands on the leader, the fish is considered whipped and caught (fair and square by their rules) even if it is released for points or if it gets away before it could be gaffed.

I know of no shark-fishing tournament that prohibits the use of firearms in dispatching a shark after it has been brought to gaff although almost all game-fish tournaments prohibit the use of firearms in dispatching fish. The officials draw the line on fish but *will* allow sharks to be dispatched with firearms. Even the Metropolitan Miami Fishing Tournament, the world's largest and one of the oldest contests with thousands of participating anglers, allows the use of firearms in dispatching sharks after they have been brought to gaff.

Unfortunately, the I.G.F.A. doesn't see it this way. Since they consider only six species of sharks as game fish, the rule prohibiting the use of firearms applies to both fish and sharks. So if you are contemplating fishing for an official world-record shark, better leave the gunpowder at home!

A shark gun is known by other names such as a "powerhead" or "bangstick." Basically, it is a short firing chamber mounted at one end of a long pole that can accommodate a 12-gauge shotgun shell. It is designed to fire underwater and uses a plastic-type waterproof shell.

To function properly, the chamber must make a forcible contact against the shark underwater. The shell detonates and the shark is usually immobilized by the combined forces of water, gas, and pellet shot, a light field load being more effective. A brain or spine shot will paralyze its entire nervous system completely, making the capture safe and easier.

Some models have interchangeable heads or chambers permitting the use of other small-but-powerful caliber shells. Every model is equipped with an "on-off" safety device. The handle ordinarily meas-

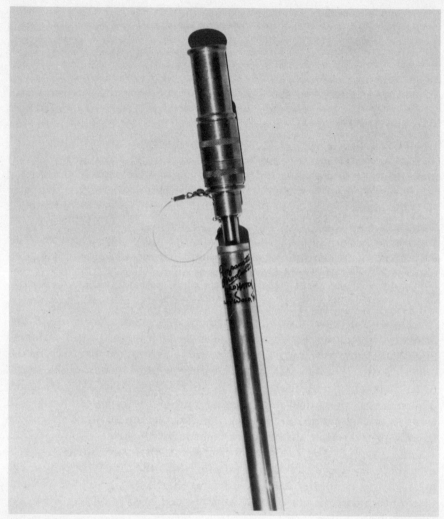

An underwater powerhead, known as a "shark gun," is a safe and practical way to dispatch a large shark quickly. The gun uses plastic-type 12-gauge shells and comes with a five- or ten-foot handle. Although it is a lethal weapon, no permit is required for its use. (Courtesy Pompanette Products, Inc.)

ures five to six feet in length but some models feature an attachment that makes the handle 10 feet long. Although all models are considered lethal weapons, no permit is required for their use. For safety, the chamber end should always be pointed away from people or objects and the safety device released only before plunging it into the water against the shark's body.

Other firearms such as pistols and rifles are often used by sharkers to finish off large sharks. However, I question their effectiveness when

Administering the coup de grace *to a shark with an underwater powerhead makes the capture easier and safer.*

compared to a shark gun. They can do a fine job if the person using them is a good marksman and is able to dispatch a shark with a minimum number of shots. A slightly wounded shark can still put up a lot of fuss and require much more time to land. The risk of losing it is still greater when poor marksmanship is responsible.

For personal reasons, some shark anglers may not wish to use firearms. If this is the case, then the best way to land a shark is with the use of a flying gaff. This is the same kind of landing equipment used in landing other large game fish such as marlin, swordfish, tuna, and giant sea bass.

Flying gaffs are made in several sizes and the smart sharker will have at least two sizes (medium and large) on board at all times. A flying gaff consists of two separate pieces held together by a light line that will break when the gaff hook is implanted into the shark. The gaff hook, secured to a stout nylon line ½ or ⅝ of an inch in diameter, disengages from the handle socket after the shark is gaffed. This allows the user to hold the shark without the rigid gaff handle.

Once the fly-gaff hook has been implanted properly, a thrashing shark is helpless and seldom gets away. Then the crew can hand-line the shark to the side of the boat where it is landed or bludgeoned to death by several (usually many) smart blows on the head with a heavy instrument such as a lead pipe or baseball bat. A meat hook is then thrust into the jaws of the shark, secured to the block and tackle attached to the gin pole, and hoisted up so that the head and trunk are well clear of the water. A safety rope should be tied around the shark's tail to secure it in the event that the shark revives and begins to lash its tail.

Fly-gaff hooks, like shark-fishing hooks, should be needle sharp and triangulated to permit easier entry into the shark's mouth or tough skin. If possible, the best place to gaff a shark is in the mouth where some control of its head and snapping jaws can be exercised. Otherwise, if the gaff is planted elsewhere in the body, the shark will dive or thrash about and the job of subduing it becomes harder and the risk of losing it is greater.

Another important piece of landing equipment is the tail rope, a special piece of gear that helps secure a vigorous shark. Tail ropes can be handmade or factory made. An ideal tail rope consists of about 10 feet of plastic-covered stainless steel cable (3/16 inch in diameter) with a large bronze snap attached to one end and about eight feet of ½-inch nylon line at the other.

The skillful use of a tail rope can immobilize almost any size shark but is not recommended without the use of a flying gaff or shark gun. The tail rope can be used in two ways—either restraining the shark's midsection (behind the pectoral fins) or securing its tail so that it can be towed backwards in an attempt to drown it.

To hold the shark's midsection, a running noose is formed out of the plastic-covered cable (the cable, in this case, is used for weight so it will sink in the water) looped around the leader, and snapped in place. The loop is then passed over the shark's head and pectoral fins where it is drawn up tight over the midsection and then snubbed to the side of the boat. The tail can be secured in the same manner.

If firearms are not used, a fly-gaff is the best way to land a large shark. The gaff hook, secured to a stout line, disengages from the handle after the hook is firmly implanted in the shark. This enables the user to hold the shark without the rigid gaff handle.

Once the loop is passed over the tail, it can be drawn tight at the caudal peduncle (the narrow section of the shark's body located forward of the tail assembly).

Fighting a large shark can be hard work regardless of how skillful an angler is. Since it may require hours to land a sizable shark, comfort and efficient fighting gear are certainly important prerequisites in this rugged sport. Modern fighting chairs, equipped with a gimbel socket

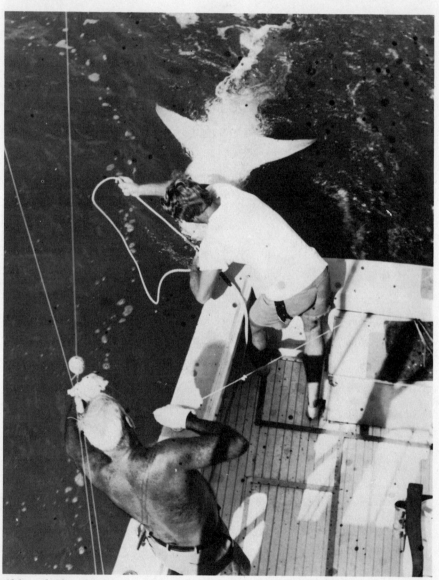

Although the skillful use of a tail rope can secure most sharks, its exclusive use is not recommended—especially on large and frisky specimens. Once the weighted running noose is snapped around the leader, the loop can then be passed over the shark's head or midsection, drawing it up tight and snubbing it to the side of the boat.

and footrests, enable the angler to achieve more leverage. A harness made of soft leather removes most of the strain from the arms and allows the angler to use his back and leg muscles while fighting a shark. Harness straps are equipped with snaps that clip to the reel lugs, allowing the angler to lean back and use his whole body while pulling on a stubborn shark.

The selection of a rod and reel depends entirely upon the angler's preference for the size shark he wants and how much skill he wishes to apply. If he likes to catch big sharks on light tackle, naturally he won't need heavy gear. Some anglers are not interested in spending a lot of time whipping a shark on light tackle only to lose it. Others, because of budget reasons, just want to get in the action and score quickly with the critters. So, I am not making any specific rod-and-reel recommendations. Each angler, with a little thought, should be able to select his own tackle, based strictly upon his choice of action.

However, I *will* make one recommendation that I believe is most important. Poorly made rods and reels have no place in shark-fishing. They don't have to be the most expensive, but they should be durable and smooth in operation. This tackle will be a little on the expensive side but the investment will prove to be the cheapest in the long run. We're fishing for rugged, stubborn brutes that will put more strain and pressure on the equipment than most other game fish of equal size.

For general all-around fishing purposes, the perfect fishing line does not exist. Every line had drawbacks and advantages and, like a custom rod built for a specific purpose, a line should be chosen for the same reason.

The three leading lines manufactured in this country today are monofilament, nylon, and dacron. For spin and bait-casting monofilament lines are ideal since they are lighter in weight and absorb more water. However, monofilament material is far more elastic than lines made of nylon or dacron. In use, this can be a hindrance and an advantage at the same time. It depends, to some degree, upon the size of the hook used.

For example, setting the hook in the tough mouth of a shark is more difficult because of the stretch. A monofilament line acts like a long rubber band and the hook doesn't begin to "dig in" until the angler has taken in most of the stretch. On the other hand, once the shark is hooked, the line is less likely to break and can absorb more shock because of its resiliency under constant pressure.

To hook large sharks (500 pounds or more) a heavy line and a large hook must obviously be used. This means that the hook will have a large barb and that a great amount of force must be exerted to drive the hook home. Since a large shark can be more difficult to hook than a smaller one, a line made of dacron (that has little stretch) should be used. Therefore, if large sharks are to be taken on 80-pound test

Joe Olenicki and son Tom, both avid light-tackle sharkers, found a school of acrobatic black-tipped spinners. Spinner sharks of all sizes, usually found in warm shallow seas, offer the ultimate in light-tackle action.

line or stronger, dacron is the best bet and will help in the most important aspect of fishing—that of setting the hook. After the shark is hooked, only expert angling skill can make it knuckle under without depending upon the characteristics found in different lines.

For smaller sharks, especially while trolling, monofilament lines of 50-pound test and under will stretch because of water friction on the line plus the slight drag created by the pull of the bait. Thus, some of the stretch is eliminated in the line,, making it suitable for setting the hook and for maintaining pressure on the shark.

If an angler is fishing for an official world-record shark, he will have to pay particular heed to line test specifications. Most lines will test greater than the manufacturer specifies on the spool. For this reason, an angler must insist upon using the special I.G.F.A. line that is guaranteed to break at exactly the specified test or slightly less than that indicated on the spool. Many anglers have caught record sharks only to have their catches disqualified because the submitted line samples tested greater than that allowed in a particular line class category.

Light-tackle fishing for sharks is gaining in popularity every day. Spinfishermen, baitcasters, and flyrodders are beginning to discover the game characteristics of some shark species. One, the black-tipped shark, is small, yet it presents a great challenge to the light-tackle buffs.

9
These Are the Champs

In this chapter, I have compiled a number of short profiles of some of the leading I.G.F.A. World Record holders; they are proficient anglers who have earned their positions in the "hall of fame."

I enjoyed corresponding with these champs who share my interest in shark-fishing. They were most cooperative in providing me with the information and photos necessary to present an accurate portrayal of their extraordinary achievements. Some were so enthusiastic that they even revealed their closely-guarded secrets. With their permission, I am happy to include these hard-earned techniques in the profiles.

Some of these champs have written their own "blow-by-blow" accounts of their great struggles with record-breaking sharks. These, too, I have included (set forth deliberately in quotes, since they reflect the honest excitement that occurred during the heat of battle!)

You can't say that one is a better angler than another; each has his own specialty. Some have developed special skills using light tackle while others are proficient with only medium or heavy tackle. All are experts. The skills of these anglers are diversified and each has achieved a high degree of sensitivity in developing his own techniques. That is why many line-test categories are necessary and made available by the I.G.F.A. so that it can embrace *all* the potential skill that exists in our vast fraternity of anglers.

So these are the champs, men and women whose skills, persistence, and spostsmanship catapulted them into fame and made them the envy of all anglers.

Alfred Dean has come a long way since the days when he used to fish for "tiddlers" along the banks of the River Murray in South Australia. His tackle at that time consisted of a homemade rod of bamboo, a piece of cotton line, and a penny hook. He didn't realize then that he was destined to become a world-famous, big-game fisherman. He

Lord Norrie, former governor general of New Zealand, with the jaws of his 2,225-pound white shark caught in 1951. Lord Norrie's catch was, at that time, the largest ever landed with rod and reel! (Courtesy Ernest Palmer)

never imagined that only a short distance away, where the waters of the River Murray emptied into the Great Australian Bight, he would be making angling history and breaking world records for catching the largest game fish known to man—the great man-eating white shark.

Dean has established seven world records for catching the largest game fish anywhere, a distinction no other angler in the world can claim. He also has the honor of landing the first official record fish on rod and reel that weighed more than a ton. This event took place in 1952 when he captured a 2,333-pounder on 130-pound test line.

Not content with some of his achievements, he even smashed his own records a few times. These accomplishments guaranteed his position in the I.G.F.A. record book for a long time to come. He still holds the records for the three largest game fish: 2,664 pounds on 130-pound test line, 2,344 pounds on 80-pound test line, and a 2,536-pounder on 180-pound test line. The latter is recorded officially by the I.G.F.A., but is not printed on the charts because he already holds an all-tackle record on 130-pound line.

His records made angling history but official records tell only part of the story. He has whipped and landed giant sharks, some of which have exceeded his present official records by more than 1,000 pounds. However, due to the many restrictions that make up the strict requirements set forth in the rules of the I.G.F.A., Dean had to disqualify himself in the interests of honesty and sportsmanship.

Dean was deadly serious about this shark-fishing business. He was only after the big ones and that meant hunting the most feared monsters of them all—the great man-eating white shark. Declared a game fish by the I.G.F.A., the weight of a white shark can exceed that of the largest true fish, the black marlin, by thousands of pounds. As the rod-and-reel records show, Dean's fantastic 2,664-pound shark exceeds the present black marlin record by more than 1,100 pounds!

Like Bob Dyer, another famous record-holder, Dean admits modestly that a lucky last-minute decision was responsible for his world-record catch in 1959. He had just completed a shark-fishing cruise with his partner, Ken Puckridge. They had already dismantled and packed their gear with the intention of returning to port when, on impulse, they decided to spend their last night anchored about a mile-and-a-half offshore. At 4:00 A.M., the all-tackle, world-record shark began knocking on Dean's door by "hitting the boat with a thud that shook it from stem to stern." Dean scrambled into action and after a grueling battle that lasted several hours, he landed the monster. It measured 16 feet, 10 inches in length, and had a girth of 9 feet, 6 inches!

Like all fishermen, Dean too has had his share of bad luck. His encounter with what he estimated conservatively as a 4,000-pounder is considered one of his most terrific struggles. This epic battle took place in 1954, when he hooked and fought a brute that was a potential

Alfred Dean of Australia, framed by the jaws of one of his world-record white sharks. Dean has captured seven world records for the largest game fish caught anywhere, a distinction no other angler in the world can claim. (Courtesy Australian Outdoors)

record for five and one-half hours, and then lost it when the hooks pulled out. After three and one-half hours, intense cramps began to develop in Dean's arms and legs. Even his powerful hands, toughened by years of gardening, were now blistered. Still, he held on stubbornly

Alfred Dean and his I.G.F.A. All-Tackle World Record white shark caught in 1959. The monster weighed 2,664 pounds and measured almost 17 feet!

because he felt that history was in the making.

"He was a tough customer," Dean claimed, "I gave him all I had and he gave me the toughest battle I have ever had. He was only hooked in the mouth yet he took our 36-foot cutter 12 miles during the fight!"

In 1961, Dean lost another monster estimated at 3,500 pounds. Knowing that there were some extremely big whites in the area, he set out to break his own record of 2,536 pounds on 180-pound line. After he had the brute on his line for 90 minutes it was ready for gaffing.

"As we were pulling him up, he rolled himself up in the trace until he came to the line, slashed it with one sweep of his great tail and was off," Dean said.

"He was really hungry. Before I had a chance to get another bait in the water, this 18-footer had grabbed three great chunks of meat from a porpoise we had tied at the stern of the boat and disappeared."

Dean remembers vividly his first encounter with a white shark back in 1939. He admits that he had only a rough idea of the kind of equipment he needed to catch monster sharks. He had fashioned his own rod and was anxious to try it out.

He chartered a boat out of Port Lincoln for a ten-day shark-fishing excursion. His skipper, Jimmy Green, chided him about the home-made rod, believing it was too weak for sharks. But Dean was determined to use it after all the time spent in building it.

On their first day out they had begun fishing 18 miles from port. The wind freshened and rough seas forced them to turn about and settle down in the lee of an island where an occasional shark had been sighted and caught.

> We were below getting lunch when *crash*—something hit the cutter. We bounded up the stairs to see the monster which Jim estimated at about 1,000 pounds.
>
> I was soon sitting in the chair, ready to bait the shark. I remember that my knees were knocking and I was shaking all over. About ten minutes after baiting this fellow, my "beautiful" cane pole gave way with a crash. Then I realized why Jim didn't think much of my gear.
>
> Jim got a broom handle and lashed it in four places above and below the break, ready for the next attack should it come.
>
> Lunch was disturbed again as we felt another thud. This time the reconstructed rod was as stiff as a piece of water pipe but at least I managed to get the shark to the boat, Jim taking the trace. It is still hard to explain, the thrill of landing that first shark. It is something I'll never forget. At Port Lincoln we found that it weighed 868 pounds.

After many years of sharking, Dean acquired a thorough knowledge of this specialized sport that requires skill, strength, a sensitive touch, and an understanding of the peculiarities of sharks. What techniques *does* an angler use to attract and hook giant sharks? Dean is generous in his advice and reveals freely what some anglers would consider well-guarded secrets:

> Well, the bait is not dropped into the shark's mouth as some people may think. Lures of porpoise, seal, or whole meat attached to ropes are

hung over the stern just touching the water.

When a shark arrives at the boat, it is allowed to take one lure. Then the rest of the lures are pulled high out of the reach of the shark, all except one which is left in the same position as the one taken by the shark.

A shark will always return to the same spot hoping for more. The baited hooks are placed on the outer position so that the shark picks the bait up on its return for the other lure.

Should it miss, then the lure is quickly pulled up and dropped back again waiting for the shark's return.

When the shark takes the bait it is usually allowed to have the lure. The shark in swallowing the lure, pushes the hooks down and they sink in.

When a shark realizes that it is hooked, the fun begins. It usually makes a run of about 200 yards, rolls on the surface and throws itself out of the water to break free.

Should it succeed in rolling the trace around it, the line will be cut, and this is when sharks are lost.

Dean has recently retired from the strenuous activity of fighting monster sharks. To look at this robust, teak-tough gardener, it is hard to believe that he doesn't want to smash any more records. The man is built like a rock, but, as he so candidly puts it, "I'm getting on in years and have more or less given the chaps away as they are getting to be hard work."

Dictionaries define *dean* as a "senior member of any body" and Alfred Dean is undisputably the dean of shark fishermen. He lives up to his name, which is synonymous with his position in the angling fraternity. His rise to this exalted position did not come easily. His many epic battles with man-eating sharks are legendary. It also meant a lot of sweat, blisters, bruises, perseverance, skill, tears, and above all, sportsmanship. These are the qualities that go into the making of a true champion.

For years, Bob and Dolly Dyer of Australia have been famous show-business personalities as well as the world's most celebrated big-game fishing team. Together they hold more official Australian and world records than any other husband-wife angling combination. Moreover, to top off this remarkable achievement, each of them is the proud possessor of more world records than any other individual angler.

The Dyers began their personal war on sharks during the early fifties. It started out as a kind of personal, exclusive adventure for them but lasted nearly ten years. They did fish for other big game occasionally, but the challenge of fishing for man-eating monsters always took first place.

The I.G.F.A. World Record charts reveal their imposing angling achievements. The name Dyer appears with such regularity that the reader might find it monotonous and assume that the contests were between two persons only. However, the records are overwhelmingly impressive, and even the casual reader is affected.

Bob and Dolly Dyer, Australia's famous show-business personalities, are also the world's most celebrated big-game fishing team. The Dyers have been credited with 13 I.G.F.A. World Record sharks caught on various line tests. Many of these records are still unbroken.

According to the 1971 I.G.F.A. World Record charts, Bob holds six records while Dolly is credited with seven. Most of these sensational catches have withstood the challenges of anglers since 1957. Even some of their earlier catches back in 1953, when they were just beginning to get their teeth into the sport, are still on the books.

Years ago, before the passage of the I.G.F.A. ruling prohibiting the use of mammal flesh and blood to attract fish or sharks, competition was keen as hundreds of anglers developed an intense interest in pursuing monster sharks and battling them for hours on end in their endeavors to garner an I.G.F.A. World Record.

These shark anglers knew that sharks are greatly attracted to mammal flesh and blood. Whaling stations were active in those days and hordes of sharks would habitually follow the towed carcasses of harpooned whales to port where they greedily gorged themselves. Sharks swiftly develop a taste for whale flesh and can pick up the irresistible scent of whale blood miles away.

It might have been a simple matter to obtain the bait and chum from the whaling stations and proceed to fish in waters that were usually populated with hungry sharks. However, it was not so simple to capture these vicious monsters on regulation tackle and accomplish this feat safely at the same time. Skillful angling and boat-handling techniques, using all safety precautions, together with an unlimited amount of stamina and energy are required to subdue these brutes. In addition, constant vigilance is also necessary to prevent other sharks from mutilating a potential record catch. It is a hectic, dangerous sport that can bring tears of joy or bitter discouragement to the angler. He and his crew must be on guard at all times and practice extreme safety measures against possible injury. Aching backs, torn ligaments, bleeding cuts, and blisters are common, but in some instances injuries can be serious enough to put an end to the grueling sport for some careless anglers.

By the late fifties, competition for the world-record white sharks was intense. Dyer's biggest competition was Alfred Dean, a real pro, who persistently fished the waters of Streaky Bay many miles away across the Great Australian Bight. Twice Dean and Dyer have taken the most coveted record (the largest shark), away from each other. At present, Dean holds the record with his 2,664-pounder on 130-pound test line.

One day Dyer came close to upsetting Dean's long-standing record with a monster that would surely have exceeded 3,000 pounds. Although Dyer modestly claims a lot of his angling success was due to good luck, he has had his share of bad luck too—bad enough to prevent him from topping Dean's enviable record. Dyer tied into one of the largest white sharks ever caught on rod and reel only to have it disqualified for the record because of mutilation by other sharks.

He had fought the giant creature for six grueling hours and finally brought it to gaff. Darkness and stormy weather set in, preventing him from bringing his potential record catch to the official weighing scales that were miles away. He and his crew spent the night in a protected

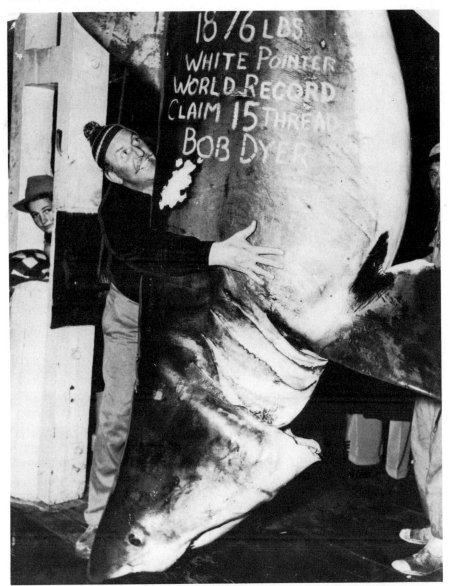

Bob Dyer fondly embraces his 1,876-pound white shark caught in 1955 on 50-pound test line. This I.G.F.A. World Record shark is believed to be the heaviest game fish ever caught in this line class.

harbor waiting for daybreak and calmer weather. Meanwhile other hungry sharks threatened to attack his shark hanging lifelessly from the side of his boat. To protect his hard-earned prize from the marauders, Dyer stood vigil with a spotlight and a .303 caliber rifle.

Unfortunately, at 2:00 A.M., his body weary and his eyes heavy with sleep, he relaxed his guard for a few minutes to have a cup of coffee. While in the cabin he heard a commotion in the water and the sickening crunch of a shark attacking his great white. Immediately he turned his spotlight on the scene and winced painfully at what he saw. The liver from his shark was torn and dangling from its underbelly. Dyer's battle with the shark had been a success but the second contest, in which he was not a participant, had ended in automatic disqualification.

Bob's wife, Dolly, has had her share of bad luck, too. Once, in 1953 she fought and landed a tiger shark that would have topped all records for tigers taken by a man or woman at that time. With precision timing and great stamina, she brought it to gaff in the incredible time of one hour and five minutes. This was an exceptional angling achievement, especially for the distaff side! After whipping her tiger into submission, she had to spend considerable time fighting off other sharks that wanted to dissect her potential record catch. It took ten hours to bring the man-eater to an official weighing station. Finally, just before weigh-in at the dock, the dead tiger, as if in revenge, began to tremble and convulse. She went into labor and began to give birth to her young. One at a time, 40 little pups wiggled out into the world! The loss of this extra weight was enough to cost Dolly her well-earned record for both men and women, but its eventual weight of 1,314 pounds earned her the world title in the 130-pound line class of the women's division of the I.G.F.A. She also holds the record of 1,052 pounds for a white shark, caught in 1954 on 130-pound line. Neither record has been broken.

Bob and Dolly have given up the strenuous grind and nerve-wracking business of chasing and fighting giant sharks. Sharking was a pioneering phase in their lives that is now past history. Subduing huge sharks using what most people would consider flimsy-looking tackle, they came close to defying the laws of physics as they whipped these monsters on threadlike lines.

When the Dyers participated in their sharking activities, the I.G.F.A. had permitted the use of any mammal flesh to attrack fish and sharks. Later, when the association ruled against using flesh, the Dyers, with true sportsmanship, endorsed the new ruling.

At present, they are still active in big-game fishing circles and enjoy traveling around the world exploring the potential in other areas.

Bob is a committee member of several international tournaments, a life member of the famous Sydney Game Fishing Club, and a member of the Board of Governors of the Hawaiian International Billfish Tournament.

The saga of their shark-hunting odyssey remains a legend in angling history. No other couple has been able to upset their records. Nor has any couple contributed so much enthusiasm and publicity to this vigorous and often dangerous sport. Their phenomenal success with fish and sharks has been recorded in literature, on film, and has been instrumental in creating worldwide interest in shark fishing.

Bob and Dolly Dyer are two of the most skillful anglers around. After years of tears and experience they have learned their skills well and met their many challenges with enthusiasm and sportsmanship. The record speaks for itself!

Walter Maxwell of Charlotte, North Carolina, has the honor of holding the official world's record for the largest tiger shark. Coincidentally, this terrific angling feat established his tiger as the largest game fish ever caught in the western hemisphere!

Maxwell is in the masonry construction business. He is a big man, 40 years old, well built and rugged as the bricks he uses in his business. He has fished all his life, catching many marlin and blue-fin tuna but preferring the rugged fight and resistance of big tiger sharks. He has learned the mysterious ways of sharks—how to break their spirit and gauge their resistance to capture—techniques that come only after many experiences with the big ones.

Maxwell has an intense interest in the feeding habits and migratory movements of sharks and keeps a record of his observations after each fishing excursion. For the past ten years he has explored the shark-fishing potential along the southeast coast of the United States and believes that the largest tiger shark population exists from May through August along the South Carolina coast. During that period, many big female tigers, heavy with upborn pups, move into shallow waters to feed and give birth to their young. From dissections made on many catches, he discovered that big tigers devour lemon sharks, skates, and stingrays. So he always tries to use a three- or four-foot lemon for bait when he suspects that a big tiger is in the area.

Maxwell's I.G.F.A. all-tackle record shark weighed 1,780 pounds, measured 13 feet, 10½ inches long, and had a girth of 103 inches. He caught this brute in 1964 from a pier at Cherry Grove, North Carolina. His catch eclipsed the old record of 1,432 pounds caught in 1958 off Cape Moreton, Australia.

Exceptional skill, strength, and special techniques were required to capture monsters from the Cherry Grove pier. Instead of battling the giants from a maneuverable boat with a comfortable fighting chair, an angler had to hook and fight his quarry standing up. When his prize was brought close to the pier, a fly-gaff and tail rope had to be secured with swift precision before the shark and line became entangled in the pier supports.

Maxwell caught his record tiger in this manner. Near the end of the long battle, he said his prayers. He wasn't sure if he could hold out much longer against this tremendous beast that refused to give up.

*Walter Maxwell and his 1,780-pound world-record tiger shark, which is offi-
cially the largest game fish ever caught on rod and reel in the western hemisphere. The I.G.F.A. all-tackle tiger was caught from a pier in Cherry Grove,
North Carolina.*

His arms and back ached with fatigue. Blood trickled down his back
where his harness cut deep into his flesh. Over a hundred spectators
cheered him on.

Finally, after fighting his tiger for three and one-half grueling hours
in the blazing heat of a summer afternoon, his prize was gaffed and
secured. Since it was too heavy to lift, it had to be maneuvered along
the length of the pier and hauled up on the beach. Local sportsmen,
sensing that he had a potential record, persuaded Maxwell to enter his
claim with the I.G.F.A. The impressive catch made newspaper headlines and congratulations poured in from all parts of the country.
Many of the local residents were pleased to see their beaches rid of
a serious threat to swimmers.

Unfortunately, some of Cherry Grove's community leaders felt differently about this remarkable angling achievement and were shaken
when they learned that such large man-eating sharks inhibited their
waters. They also feared that Maxwell's record catch might encourage
more shark-fishing and it did. Hundreds of anglers converged on

Cherry Grove trying to beat Maxwell's record. Believing that this could create some adverse publicity which might prove detrimental to their tourist business, the legislators voted to prohibit shark-fishing from their pier and beaches.

One day, Maxwell met his match—or his tackle did—since he claims that he could have beaten the monster if he had been fishing from a boat. At the time, however, he was fishing from another pier. (This always hinders an angler's movements when fighting his quarry, and reduces his chances of capturing an exceptionally large shark.) Maxwell had hooked into what he had estimated to be at least a 2,500-pound tiger. In 15 minutes, he was helpless and was left holding an empty reel. The brute had made one long run, taking all of Maxwell's line with it. Some mighty salty language filled the air and since then, Maxwell has fished from a boat!

On another occasion, while battling with a 1,200-pound tiger, Maxwell spotted the largest shark he had ever seen. The giant zeroed in on Maxwell's hooked tiger, attacked (taking a large chunk out of it), and then disappeared. Maxwell brought his tiger in and examined the huge gaping wound, measuring 36 inches across. Judging from its size and shape of the tooth marks, he estimated that the attack may have been made by a white shark that would have weighed at least 3,500 pounds!

Like Alf Dean in far-off Australia (holder of a world's record for the largest white shark), Maxwell is meticulous and fussy with his fishing equipment. He files his hooks to a triangular point creating three sharp cutting edges for more efficient penetration. His tackle is the finest available and he uses the largest reel made, a 16/0 Penn that can hold 1,000 yards of 130-pound test line.

Maxwell belongs to that special group of sharkers scattered throughout the world who are consumed with a compulsion to whip ferocious sea-going mammoths on tackle geared to capture only moderately sized game. He fishes from his own boat now, and plies the waters of the continental shelf off South Carolina hunting only for the big tigers. Presently, he is faced with the supreme challenge—that of breaking his own record. Chances are good that some day he will.

The formation of shark-fishing clubs throughout the British Channel Islands has helped local anglers to band together and charter a large boat in their quest for the bigger sharks that usually inhabit offshore waters.

One club, known as the 30 Fathoms Club of Guernsey, has made newspaper headlines because of the recent angling achievement of Des Bougourd, one of its newly subscribed members.

It was during one of the club's yearly outings when they ventured well offshore that Bougourd connected with a world-record porbeagle

A new all-time Metropolitan Miami Fishing Tournament record. Robert M. Mostler of Lake Worth, Florida, caught the 1,007-pound great hammerhead shark at Grassy Key, Florida Keys. The 15-foot monster was so big that it had to be chopped in three pieces before it could be weighed.

shark that made the Channel Islands appear much larger on the map.

Bougourd, relatively new to the strenuous and tricky sport of big-game sharking, proved himself a pro by copping two I.G.F.A. world records, one in the all-tackle division and another in the 80-pound test line division. In addition, he marched away with two British records previously held by members of the Shark Angling Club of Great Britain.

As a further tribute to his exceptional angling feat, he was rewarded with several trophies and various kinds of fishing equipment by proud Britons throughout the islands.

For two and a half hours Bougourd skillfully kept the pressure on a swift, streamlined sea-going engine while standing up during the entire struggle. Bougourd's battle with his record porbeagle is indeed a classic.

Sharks are sometimes caught under unusual circumstances. Not all world-record sharks were caught by anglers who fished for them with

This I.G.F.A. World Record 430-pound porbeagle shark was caught off Britain's Channel Islands by Desmond Bougourd. (Courtesy Brian J. Green, Channel Islands)

the express intention of breaking existing records. Some were caught quite by accident while the angler was searching for other game fish.

One such ludicrous incident took place seven years ago when Captain Ray Acord tangled with an uninvited shark. Acord, an enthusiastic angler who prefers to fish with light tackle, had set his sights on breaking the world record for striped marlin using 12-pound test line.

He was fishing off the coast of Mazatlan, Mexico, when he hooked a striped marlin. As the marlin began to execute its spectacular leaps, Acord was convinced that he was tied to a record-breaker. Sometime during the tussle, the marlin threw the hook and disappeared while the still-intact bait was swallowed immediately by a white shark. Not knowing that a switch had been made, Acord continued his struggle with his record "marlin."

It was not until 45 minutes later, when his quarry finally surfaced, that Acord discovered his marlin had become a shark. For a moment he was angry enough to cut the leader in disgust. Then, however, he was forced to acknowledge that this shark had given him a good fight and had fooled him completely with its true game qualities.

This prompted him to bring it in for official weighing, suspecting that a record for 12-pound test line was in the offing. Later, he was pleased to learn that he had unintentionally broken a world record with a 96-pound, 10 ounce white shark!

A common practice when fishing for sharks from a boat in Australian waters, is to criss-cross the wake of a slow-moving commercial fishing vessel. Sharks have frequently been known to follow these vessels for miles, waiting patiently for fish remains or to make a grab for the trapped fish that are struggling in the nets.

On March 27, 1967, Barry Caldwell's skipper did just that. They were trolling with striped mackerel in the wake of a trawler when they got the strike that gave Caldwell a world record.

Something grabbed his bait and sounded immediately, running off several hundred yards of line. It was not until the creature surfaced for the first time that Caldwell realized that he had tied on to a huge thresher shark that was flailing its great tail and sending spray in all directions.

The astounded crew, now hysterical with joy, assured Caldwell that he had a winner and, with their encouragement, he buckled down for a fight just as the monster sounded again. It was a strenuous and protracted struggle but he soon forgot his aching muscles as he finally brought his prize alongside for gaffing. At this point, the water boiled as the thresher exploded into a last furious effort to free itself. Caldwell was terrified for a moment but relaxed when the gaff struck home.

As the cruiser headed for Port Stephens and the official weighing scales, Caldwell had little time to muse over the prospects of becoming

Joe Skala proudly admires his prize-winning lemon shark. Skala brought the 250-pounder to gaff in less than a half hour and won a citation for his angling achievement despite his handicap.

a record-holder. But the scales told the story—501 pounds—a new world's record on 80-pound test line!

During the late fifties, Del Marsh used to comb the waters of California's Long Beach Harbor searching diligently for sharks. He still continues this practice, but hasn't been able to top his own 92½ pound I.G.F.A. World Record thresher caught in 1959 in 12-pound test line. Although many other anglers have tried to snatch the record from him, all have failed. Some have come mighty close.

Marsh is an expert light-tackle angler and, after years of whipping big sharks on fine gossamerlike line, he had learned about the obscure laws of physics that come into play when fishing for heavy game.

He also learned that drifting a bait instead of trolling is a better way to connect with threshers. He would scan the skies and water intently watching for gulls feeding upon the surface, usually indicating that a school of bait fish is near. He discovered that nature intended the thresher to use its huge tail as a whip to stun these schooled bait fish. The thresher then turns around and gobbles the stunned fish left in its wake. Every time Marsh spotted this signpost of action, he would run over and begin another drift with his bait. His keen observation and patience usually paid off. He experimented with different baits and the methods of presenting them. He studied the erratic move-

Del Marsh, a light-tackle buff from California, caught this 92½-pound thresher shark on 12-pound test line. His outstanding achievement earned an I.G.F.A. World Record.

ments of threshers as they migrated from season to season; he discovered some of their favorite haunts. In other words, Marsh worked hard at the sport and eventually became an expert.

Marsh knew that he was coming close to catching some world-record threshers in the different line categories and decided to "post one on the board." He studied the International Game Fish Association record book and rules and found his challenge waiting for him. He discovered an opening for threshers in the 12-pound test line category. Now his interest in thresher fishing took on a new meaning and he was becoming obsessed with the capture of a record. He was putting out to sea in pursuit of threshers at every opportunity.

One day, he hooked up with what he knew must be a record. After a two-hour struggle, he brought it alongside for gaffing. It was so immense that his assistant, who was supposed to handle the gaff, refused to tackle the job of boating it. According to I.G.F.A. rules, they could use only a gaff hook or tail rope. Finally, Marsh had to break off the shark and go in search of another gaff man to assist him.

Naturally, he was disappointed, but he was far from being discouraged. Now he knew that he was sitting on top of some hot thresher action and the possibility of a shot at a world record stimulated him. He returned to port, found another assistant to handle the gaff, and proceeded immediately to the same area hoping to "strike while the iron was still hot"!

It was hot all right, for in a matter of minutes Marsh struck another thresher and his delicate 12-pound line began to disappear from his reel with lightning rapidity. Marsh and his mate were forced to start their boat and follow the thresher to recover line.

The chase took them into the midst of one of the annual boat races at Long Beach. The thresher began to jump directly in the middle of the race course! Delighted spectators had a double show to watch, but not for long. The officials stopped the race so that everyone could see the contest. This allowed Marsh to finish his "race," capture his thresher, and post an all-time record in the book!

When Doug Ross of New Zealand (on leave from the Air Force) latched on to his 1,000 pound mako in 1943, he had no idea that he was tied into an I.G.F.A. all-tackle record that would stand unbroken for 27 years.

Big-game fishing had always been Ross's favorite sport; he was an old hand at whipping sharks, marlin, and tuna. But landing this record-breaker on 130-pound test line was like a dream come true. He captured the brute off Mayor Island, New Zealand, one of the old fishing haunts of Zane Grey, the famous big-game angler and writer of Westerns.

Ross and his friends had chartered a big-game fishing launch for a

*Doug Ross of New Zealand had no idea that his 1,000-pound mako shark
would remain an all-tackle I.G.F.A. World Record catch for 27 years.*

day of marlin-fishing when a strange event took place. One of his companions had hooked and brought to gaff a striped marlin. To their
surprise, a huge mako appeared and, before the marlin could be boated, seized the marlin's entire tail section, completely severing it. The

crew managed to boat the marlin before the hungry mako could continue its vicious assault. In anger, the mako cruised around fearlessly in the blood-stained water, making an occasional grab at the stern of the launch.

After making a rough estimate of its size, Ross knew then that he wanted the brute badly. He grabbed a rod as one of the crew rigged a Kawhai (local bait fish) and tossed it to the enraged shark. In an instant, the mako had the bait and hook firmly planted in its mouth.

The mako sounded several times, tearing out hundreds of yards of line. Finally, after a two-hour struggle, Ross expertly brought it alongside the launch for gaffing. All seven hands strained to lift the mako aboard but found it too heavy. It looked like a winner so they towed it back to port for an official weight.

Unfortunately, the only available scales were limited to 1,000 pounds. Ross's heavy mako exceeded the limit as the machine came to an abrupt stop. Unable to make any other weighing arrangements, Ross was forced to accept the official 1,000 pound reading without really knowing the true weight of his prize. On-the-spot observers estimated that the brute would weigh at least 200 to 300 pounds more.

Big makos are both tough and scarce and it was not until 27 years later that Ross's record was finally broken by another weighing 1,061 pounds that now has the lead in the I.G.F.A. all-tackle record book. Many anglers believe that, if Ross's mako had been weighed on a larger scale, he would still hold the record today and, possibly, for many years to come.

Regardless of the unfortunate limitation of the scales, Ross held a record for one of the longest periods in the history of the I.G.F.A.!

10

The International Game Fish Association

THE INTERNATIONAL GAME FISH ASSOCIATION (AFFILIATED WITH THE American Museum of Natural History) is the official arbiter and re- corder of world-record game fish catches. It is a unique, nonprofit organization whose purpose is to generate sportsmanship and unite the anglers of the world. It promotes the sport of saltwater fishing by regulating the methods and ethical conduct involved in pursuing and landing game fish. In other words, the I.G.F.A. lays it on the line. For a fish to be considered for a record, it must be caught strictly in ac- cordance with their rules and regulations.

Its prescribed procedures have been accepted and used as classic guides by countless angling organizations and tournaments through- out the world. This distinguished association is a smoothly run complex piece of machinery, the administrative apparatus of which reaches out into almost every foreign land where anglers soak a line in the briny. The I.G.F.A. has over 600 affiliates—member clubs and scientific in- stitutions.

Although the shark is not a true bony fish, the association recognizes six species of sharks whose game characteristics qualifies them for in- clusion in the selected list of game fishes. These are the great white (*Carcharodon carcharias*), mako (*Isurus oxyrinchus* and *I. glaucus*), blue (*Prionace. glauca*), tiger (*Galeocerdo cuvieri*), porbeagle (*Lamna nasus*), and the thresher (*Alopias vulpinus*).

As more fishermen become infected with shark fever, other species of sharks with similar game qualities should be added to this list of gamesters. Performers such as the acrobatic small black-tipped and the large black-tipped spinner sharks should be included. The bulldog tactics of the hammerheads and the stubborn resistance of the lemons and bulls, plus the fact that they are considered aggressive and highly

210

dangerous to swimmers, also makes these species potential candidates.

Just because certain sharks are particularly dangerous to swimmers does not necessarily qualify them as rod-and-reel gamesters, but anglers all over the world will attest to the game qualities of most of them. Anglers have reported that Africa's notorious killer, the Zambezi; Australia's swift gray nurse; the ferocious Ganges River shark; and the white-tipped shark have provided outstanding action and resistance to capture that far surpass the fighting qualities of many other game fish.

The number of shark species is great, something like 250 scientifically identified species with some still not clearly classified. With the exception of the few already mentiond, most of the others are either rare, too small, or just not game enough to be considered eligible for any sort of angling challenge.

It is interesting to note that, officially, the largest living creature ever caught on rod and reel was a shark. I.G.F.A. records reveal that this shark exceeded the weight of the largest game bony fish caught on rod and reel by over 1,100 pounds!

For years there has been a growing interest in the number and size of game fish and sharks that have been caught but for some reason were disqualified for an I.G.F.A. record. Naturally these fish must have been larger than the ones on record and would give us a fairly accurate picture of just how large these creatures really get.

The I.G.F.A. has recently inaugurated a program to supervise and document information on any game fish or shark that exceeds present record standings regardless of whether it has been disqualified or caught by unconventional means. These unofficial catches will be recorded and the list made available to the general public in the near future.

Anglers should find it fascinating to compare the official catches with the unofficial list of those caught by unacceptable methods. We know that the official I.G.F.A. record for the largest white shark caught on rod and reel is 2,664 pounds. We also know that whites up to 4,000 pounds were caught on rod and reel but did not qualify. Whites weighing 4,000 to 6,000 pounds have been harpooned or have been reported caught by other unconventional methods. These large sharks would be listed in the unofficial records and will certainly intoxicate anglers with the prospects of catching bigger game than they ever dreamed of for official records.

To qualify for an official I.G.F.A. record, the catch must be made in strict observance of its rules with the use of proper tackle and landing equipment. A sample of the line must be submitted for testing; photographs and notarized affidavits verifying the catch and weight must accompany the application for the claim. Anglers who believe they may be fishing for record fish should obtain a copy of the current record standings and rules by sending $1.25 to the International Game

Fish Association, 3000 E. Las Olas Blvd., Ft. Lauderdale, Florida 33316.

The men and women who are credited with record sharks are some of the real experts, the nobility of angling circles. Courage, stamina, skill, and (above all) sportsmanship are required to get on this respected and exalted roll. These are the anglers who have met the supreme challenge, anglers whose patience and endurance approached the breaking point as they engaged in a superhuman contest between man and beast—a physical struggle with ferocious marine animals using tackle that comes close to defying the laws of physics.

These are the champs, as of now. Some haven't been unseated for many years. Some have met their own challenge, and unseated themselves only to increase the competition. The many blank spaces that exist on the charts signify that, up to now, no one has been able to catch that particular species whose weight must meet I.G.F.A. requirements. There are a lot of sharks out there—big ones—waiting for admission into sharkdom's hall of fame. Good luck!

Glossary

ABEAM—In a direction 90 degrees from the centerline of a vessel. Used to refer to an object outside the vessel

APATITE—A mineral substance composed of carbonates and calcium phosphates

ASTERN—Toward the stern or at the rear of a vessel

BANGSTICK—An underwater gun whose shell detonates when the chamber comes in forcible contact with a shark's body

BEAMING—The process by which flesh is removed from the hide with the use of a beaming knife

BERLEY—Australian term for chum: ground-up whale, seal, or fish used to attract sharks

BIRDSNEST—An expression used by anglers when a fishing line becomes fouled in a reel

BLUE POINTER—Great white shark

BOLLARD—An upright wooden or metal post around which to fasten a line

BOW—The forward part of a vessel

BRIDLE—Method of securing anchor line to boat to maintain desired position in wind and current

CARDIAC STOMACH—The portion of the stomach that sorts the food before it enters the pyloric stomach

CAUDAL PEDUNCLE—That narrow part of the shark's body located forward of the tail

CENTRUM—A vertebral disc

CHINE—That portion of the hull underwater where the bottom planking meets the side planking

CHUM—Ground-up oily fish

CHUMMING—Method of presenting chum to attract fish or sharks

CHUM SLICK—Smooth water created by the oil in the chum

CHYME—Food that has been acted upon by stomach enzymes but has not yet been passed on into the intestines

CILIA—Microscopic hairlike processes

CLASPER—Penislike appendage, which is the male shark's external reproductive organ

CLEAT—A metal or wood fitting with two arms or horns on which a line can be secured

COAMING—A vertical member around cockpits, hatches, etc., to prevent water on the deck from running below

COMMENSALISM—A relationship of two creatures where only one benefits from association with the other

COURTSHIP SCARS—Injuries caused by the male shark while biting the female during mating process

DERMAL DENTICLES—Placoid scales imbedded in shark's tough skin having characteristics similar to teeth

DRAG—The adjustable mechanism in the reel that is able to brake the spool

DRIFT—The velocity of a tidal current

DRIFTING—Fishing with lines trailing in the water while the boat is moving only with the current or wind

DROP-BACK—Allowing the line to run free from the reel spool prior to engaging the brake and setting the hook

DUCTUS DEFERENS—Also known as the Wolffian duct, the coiled tube that transports the male sperm

DYNAMOMETER—Instrument to measure force or power exerted by an object

EBB—The movement of ocean water running out to sea

ECOLOGY—The science of the relationship between organisms and their environment

FETAL—Referring to the unborn

FLESHING—The process of removing flesh from the hide

FLOOD TIDE—Tidal water moving toward shore

FLYING GAFF—A piece of landing equipment consisting of a large detachable hook secured to a stout line, which is attached to a long handle

FOLLOW-UP—A curious game fish or shark hesitating before striking at a bait

FREESPOOL—A reel spool revolving freely with the brake disengaged

GENUS—A category of related organisms including several species

GIN-POLE—A wood or metal post equipped with block and tackle used to hoist heavy fish from the water

GRAVID—Pregnant

GUNWALE—Upper edge of the upper side of an open boat

HABITAT—A permanent or temporary environment of a plant or animal

I.G.F.A.—International Game Fish Association

JIG—A leaded artificial lure made of bucktail hair, feathers, nylon, or substitute material

JIGGING—A method of attracting fish by inducing erratic action while retrieving a lure

KEEL—The main longitudinal timber located at the bottom of a vessel

KNOCK-DOWN—Expression used by trollers when a game fish strikes and pulls the line from the outrigger clip

LEADER—That portion of fishing line made of wire, cable, or monofilament that is used between the main line and the bait

LIPID—Fat and fatlike substance normally present in the body

LONGLINE—A long, heavy steel cable line consisting of short lines secured to baited hooks used to catch large amounts of fish or sharks

LORENZINI'S AMPULLAE—Small pores located on a shark's head that detect changes in temperature and pressure

MENHADEN—A bait fish high in oil content. When ground up, it is called mossbunker and used for chumming purposes to attract fish

METABOLISM—The process by which foods are transformed into basic elements that can be utilized by the body for energy and growth

METASTASIS—The traveling of a disease process from one part of the body to another

MIGRATION—Seasonal move from one region to another

MONO—Nickname for monofilament line, a synthetic commonly used for fishing lines and leaders

OLFACTORY—Pertaining to the sense of smell

OSMOSIS—The process of transmitting nourishment into the blood stream through a semipermeable membrane such as the inner intestinal wall

OUTRIGGER—A long pole projecting from the side of a boat. Its function is to hold the fishing line aloft and apart from the other lines and to facilitate the drop-back technique while using an outrigger clip

OUTRIGGER CLIP—The device attached to the halyard line of the outrigger pole and holds the fishing line with measured tension, releasing it after a fish strikes

OVIPAROUS—Producing eggs that hatch outside the body

OVOVIVIPAROUS—Capable of producing eggs that hatch inside the mother's body. Further development is necessary before the young are born alive

PELAGIC—Pertaining to open oceans or seas

POWERHEAD—An underwater gun whose shell detonates when the chamber is forcibly thrust against a shark's body

PYLORIC STOMACH—That second section of the stomach which receives digestible food from the cardiac stomach

RADIOCARBON DATING—A method by which the approximate age of fossils or prehistoric organic residue is determined

RES—Reticuloendothelial system, all the phagocyte cells in the body located in the lymphatic channels, bone marrow, connective tissues, lungs, liver, adrenal glands, etc.

ROD BUTT—Handle of a fishing rod

RUBBY-DUBBY—A British expression for chum, ground fish to attract sharks

SHARKATHON—A shark-fishing tournament

SPIRACLE—Orifice located on each side of head through which water can be drawn in for breathing

SQUALENE—A fatty material made up of precholesterol molecules

STEM—A timber reaching from the forward end of the keel up to the bowsprit and to which the two sides of the vessel are secured

TAXONOMY—The science or principle of classification; the classification of organisms in categories based on common characteristics

TERMINAL RIG—The assembly that consists of the hook, leader, and swivel or snap

THERMOCLINE—That area below the surface where warmer water exists

TIDDLER—Small panfish found in the rivers and streams of South Australia

TIDE RIP—Junction where tidal currents collide with stationary or moving water

TRACE—Wire or cable leader between the fishing line and hook

TRAIL—Australian expression for a chum slick

TRANSOME—That area of planking across the stern of a boat

VIVIPAROUS—Capable of giving birth to offspring that develop completely within the mother's body

WHITE DEATH—Great white shark

WHITEPOINTER—Great white shark

YAW—The motion of a vessel as the bow and stern move from side to side in opposite directions

Bibliography

Baldridge, Jr., Captain D. A., U.S.N., and Williams, J. "Shark Attack: Feeding or Fighting?" *Military Medicine*, February 1969.

Beaumariage, D. S. *Commercial Shark Fishing and Processing in Florida.* Educational Series, no. 16., Tallahassee: Florida Board of Conservation, 1968.

Bigelow, H. B., and Schroeder, W. C. *Fishes of the Western North Atlantic, Memoir No. 1; Part One, Lancelets, Cyclostomes, Sharks.* Sears Foundation, Marine Research. Cambridge, Mass.: Yale University Press, 1948.

Bigelow, H. B.; Schroeder, W. C.; and Springer, S. "New and Little Known Sharks from the Atlantic and From the Gulf of Mexico." *Bull. Mus. Comp. Tool.* (Harvard University), 109 (July 1953): 213-276.

Bigelow, H. B., and Schroeder, W. C. *Guide to Commercial Shark Fishing in the Caribbean Area.* Fish and Wildlife Service, fishery leaflet no. 135. Washington, D.C.: U.S. Dept. Interior, 1945.

Brown, M. E. ed. *The Physiology of Fishes; Vol. 11, Behavior.* New York: Academic Press, 1957.

Butler, Jean Campbell. *Danger, Shark!* Boston: Little-Brown, 1964.

Carson, R. L. *The Sea Around Us.* London, New York: Oxford University Press, 1954.

Case, Gerard R. *Fossil Shark and Fish Remains of North America.* 1967.

Casey, J. G. *Angler's Guide to Sharks of the Northeastern United States.* Bureau of Sport Fisheries and Wildlife, cir. no. 179. Washington, D.C.: U.S. Dept. Interior, April 1964.

Clark E. *Lady With a Spear.* New York: Harper & Bros., 1953.

————. "Four Shark Attacks on the West Coast of Florida, Summer, 1958." *Copeia* 1 (1960): 63-67.

————. *The Lady and the Sharks.* New York: Harper and Row, 1969.

Clarke, J. *Man is the Prey.* New York: Stein and Day, 1969.

Colman, J. S. *The Sea and its Mysteries.* New York: Norton and Co., 1950.

Coppleson, V. M. *Shark Attack.* London: Angus & Robertson, 1959.

Cousteau, J. Y. and Dumas, F., *The Silent World.* New York: Harper & Bros., 1953; London: Hamish Hamilton, 1953.

Cromie, W. J. *The Living World of the Sea.* Englewood Cliffs: Prentice-Hall, Inc., 1966.

Davies, David H. *About Sharks and Shark Attack.* New York: Hobbs, Dorman and Co., 1966; London: Routledge & Kegan Paul Ltd., 1965.

Davies, D. H. and Campbell, G. D. "The Etiology, Clinical Pathology and Treament of Shark Attack." *Journal Royal Naval Medical Service* 48 (1962): 1-27.

Food and Agricultural Organization of the U.N. *Fisheries Yearbook.* Rome: United Nations, 1960.

Gans, C. and Parsons, T. S. *A Photographic Atlas of Shark Anatomy.* New York: Academic Press, 1964.

Gilbert, P. W.; Schultz, L. P.; and Springer, S. "Shark Attacks During 1959." *Science* 132 (1960): 323-326.

————. "The Shark: Barbarian and Benefactor." *BioScience* 18 (October 1968): 946-950.

————. The Behavior of Sharks. *Scientific American* 207 (July 1962): 60.

Gilbert, P. W.; Mathewson, R. F.; and Rall, D. P. *Sharks, Skates, and Rays.* Baltimore: The Johns Hopkins Press, 1967.

Gilbert, P .W.; ed. *Sharks and Survival.* Boston: D. C. Heath and Co., 1963.

Gray, William B. *Creatures of the Sea.* New York: Wilfred Funk, Inc., 1960.

Gruber, S., Nelson, D. "Sharks: Attraction by Low Frequency Sounds." *Science* 142 (1963): 975-977.

Halstead, B. W. *Dangerous Marine Animals.* Cambridge, Md.: Cornell Maritime Press, 1959.

Heller, J. H. *Of Mice, Men and Molecules.* New York: Scribner's Sons, 1960.

Helm, Thomas. *Shark! Unpredictable Killer of the Sea.* New York: Dodd, Mead and Co., 1961.

Kenny, N. T. "Sharks: Wolves of the Sea." *National Geographic Magazine,* February 1968, 222-257.

Lagler, L. E.; Bardach, J. E.; and Miller, R. R: *Ichthyology.* New York: John Wiley & Sons, Inc., 1962.

Lineaweaver, T. H., III, and Backus, R. H. *The Natural History of Sharks.* New York: J. B. Lippincott Co., 1970.

Mackerodt, F. "Shark Fishing." *True,* July 1971, 37-41.

Matthiessen, P. *Blue Meridian.* New York: Random House, 1971.

Maxwell, G. *Harpoon at a Venture.* London: Rubert Hart-Davis, 1952.

McClane, J. J. *McClane's Standard Fishing Encyclopedia and International Angling Guide.* New York: Holt, Rhinehart and Winston, 1965.

McCormick, Harold W.; Allen, Tom; with Young, Capt. William E. *Shadows in the Sea.* Philadelphia, Chilton Book Co., 1963.

Moss, Frank T. "The Fish Everyone Hates." *Sportfishing,* July 1967, p. 16.

Nelson, D. R., and Gruber, S. H. "Sharks: Attraction by Low-Frequency Sounds." *Science* 142 (Nov. 1963): 975.

Norman, J. R. *A History of Fishes.* New York: Hill and Wang, 1954.

O'Connor, P. F. *Shark!* New York: W. W. Norton and Co., 1954.

Phinizy, C. "The Sharks Are Moving In." *Sports Illustrated* (December 9, 1968): 68-72.

Poli, R. *Sharks Are Caught At Night.* Translated by Naomi Wilford. Chicago: Regnery Co., 1959.

Ray, C., and Ciampe, E. *The Underwater Guide to Marine Life.* New York: A. S. Barnes and Co., Inc., 1956.

Rhodes, F. H. T.; Zim, H. S.; and Shaffer, P. R. *Fossils: A Guide to Pre-historic Life.* New York: Golden Press, 1962.

Richardson, E. S., Jr. "Rare 250-Million-Year-Old Sharks Found in Indiana." *Chicago Natural History Museum Bulletin* 28 (1957): 8.

Scharp, H. *Florida's Game Fish and How to Land Them.* South Brunswick and New York: A. S. Barnes and Co., Inc., 1968.

Schultz, L. P., with Stern, E. M. *The Ways of Fishes.* New York: D. Van Nostrand Co.,1948.

Scott, J. D. "Daredevil Sport: Shark Tagging." *Sports Afield,* March 1965, p. 36-37.

Springer, S. "Oviphagous Embryos of the Sand Shark." *Copeia* 3 (1948): 153-157.

Straughan, Robert. *Sharks, Morays and Treasure.* South Brunswick and New York: A. S. Barnes and Co., Inc., 1965.

Thompson, J. R. and Springer, S. *Sharks, Skates, Rays and Chimaeras.* Fish and Wildlife Service, cir. 228. Washington, D.C.: U.S. Dept. Interior, Sept. 1965.

Travis, W. *Shark for Sale.* London: George Allen & Unwin, 1961.

U.S. Navy. *Diving Manual, Part 1.* Washington, D.C.: Navy Dept., Navships, 1959, 250-538.

U.S. Navy. *Shark Sense.* Washington, D.C.: NAVAFR 00-80Q-14, 1959.

Volpe, Alfred. "Sharks are Useful." *Sea Frontiers* 4 (Nov. 1958): 224.

Vorenberg, M. "Cannibalistic Tendencies of Lemon and Bull Sharks." *Copeia* 2 (1962): 455-456.

Watkins, A. *The Sea My Hunting Ground.* New York: St. Martin's Press, 1958.

Wise, H. D. *Tigers of the Sea.* New York: Derrydale Press, 1937.

Young, W. E., with Mazet, H. S. *Shark! Shark! The Thirty-Year Odyssey of a Pioneer Shark Hunter.* New York: Gotham House, 1934.

Zern, E., ed. *Zane Grey's Adventures in Fishing.* New York: Harper & Bros., 1952.

Index

222